Pembrokeshire Walking on the level

Norman and June Buckley

Published by Sigma Leisure – an imprint of
Sigma Press, Stobart House, Pontyclerc, Penybanc Road
Ammanford, Carmarthenshire SA18 3HP

British Library Cataloguing in Publication Data

A CIP record for this book is available from the British Library

ISBN: 978-1-85058-8

Typesetting and Design by: Sigma Press, Ammanford, Carms

Maps: © Bute Cartographics

Photographs: © June Buckley

Cover photographs: © Norman and June Buckley
Main picture: St David's Cathedral
Left to right: Carreg Samson, Cromlech, Abercastle; Tunnel at Saundersfoot; Porthgain Harbour; Cottages Abercastle

Printed by: Cromwell Group, Trowbridge, Wiltshire

Disclaimer: The information in this book is given in good faith and is believed to be correct at the time of publication. Care should always be taken when walking in hill country. Where appropriate, attention has been drawn to matters of safety. The author and publisher cannot take responsibility for any accidents or injury incurred whilst following these walks. Only you can judge your own fitness, competence and experience. Do not rely solely on sketch maps for navigation: we strongly recommend the use of appropriate Ordnance Survey (or equivalent) maps.

Preface

This is the sixth volume of the popular and well-established series of 'level walks' books. In the context of a walking guide, level cannot, of course, be taken literally; even disused railway lines have gradients and canal tow paths rise past locks! What it does mean is that in an area where there are mountains – in this case the Preselis – deep valleys and a demanding coast path, the first consideration in selecting and recommending a walk is to limit the total ascent. Additionally, within that total ascent, the length and gradient of any particular rise is taken into account. Four hundred feet or so spread over three or four miles at reasonable gradients may be acceptable. The same rise in one prolonged slope, particularly if steep, will not. Yet another factor is the type and condition of the track or footpath. Rough surfaces underfoot, awkward steps and serious mud all add difficulty to any demanding ascent or descent.

The authors continue to believe that there are many walkers and potential walkers who want to enjoy the countryside but, for whatever reason, are happy to undertake only comparatively short, easy walks with the reassurances that the effort required is known before setting out, that they will not encounter unexpected difficulties and that the route directions are clear, both in text and by sketch map.

In this series interest is added by the brief description of features encountered along the way and by recommendations for refreshment wherever possible. Pembrokeshire is particularly rich in pre-historic monuments such as cromlechs and Celtic crosses and there is also a fascinating industrial heritage at places such as Porthgain, Amroth and Stepaside. This information is set out concisely in the introduction to each of the twenty-five walks. Use of the relevant large scale map is also recommended for the added advantage of placing any particular route in its landscape context.

The Pembrokeshire Coast Path, extending for almost 200 miles from close to St Dogmael's in the north to Amroth in the south-east corner of the county, is a fine but very demanding walk; for our purposes several selected lengths have been incorporated into generally circular routes. Other designated trails in the county include the less well known Landsker Borderlands Trail and the Knights Way. Both have been used where appropriate in selecting a range of walks with maximum possible landscape diversity.

Even for these comparatively easy walks, good footwear, preferably boots, is essential; likewise, particularly along the coast path, clothing which protects against a combination of wind and rain should be worn or carried. With no route likely to occupy more than a half day, there is little need to carry more than a bare minimum of food and drink.

Whilst only one of the routes (walk 19) has a specific recommendation for the use of a bus, there are others, for example walks 5, 6, 18 and 20, in which walkers may be able to make a speedy return by bus, perhaps due to a change of weather or other unforeseen circumstances. The local bus services, including the several 'shuttles' (some of which are seasonal) are comprehensive, with timetables obtainable from Tourist Information Centres.

Norman and June Buckley
May 2010

Contents

Tourist Information Centres

St David's
Oriel y Parc
Tel: 01437 725087

Newport
Long Street
Tel: 01239 820912

Tenby
South Parade
Tel: 01834 845040

Unit 2, Upper Park Road
Tel: 01834 842404

Saundersfoot
Harbour Car Park
Tel: 01834 813672

Pembroke
The Commons Road
Tel: 01646 622388

Milford Haven
94, Charles Street
Tel: 01646 690866

Haverfordwest
Old Bridge
Tel: 01437 763110

Fishguard
The Town Hall
Tel: 01348 873484

Walk 1: Nevern

The outward section of this walk is easy, along broad tracks without much ascent. The return is a little more difficult, a generally narrower path with a few rock steps, stiles and a rise across a large field.

Nevern is a quietly charming village. The church of St Brynach has a 12ᵗʰ century tower; most of the remainder of the structure is 14ᵗʰ/15ᵗʰ century, restored in 1864. In the churchyard is one of the finest Celtic crosses (10ᵗʰ/11ᵗʰ century) in the area, rivalled only by those at Carew and Penally. The avenue of yews is believed to be 600 years old; the second yew on the right, from the churchyard entrance, has an almost continuous drip of red sap which has given rise to folklore stories concerning the alleged unjust hanging of a monk from the tree.

Outside the churchyard, the well-preserved mounting block is claimed to be one of only two remaining in Pembrokeshire. Towards the end of the walk look out carefully for an ancient Pilgrims' Cross, cut into the solid rock face on the left, with a kneeling ledge below. This was probably a pausing place on the pilgrims' route from St Dogmael's Abbey to St David's.

Distance	4 km (2½ miles)
Ascent	75m (246ft)
Maps	Ordnance Survey Explorer OL35, North Pembrokeshire, 1:25,000
Start/Parking	In Nevern village, limited spaces off road, grid reference 082400. Large car park (for customers) at Trewern Arms Inn
Refreshments:	Trewern Arms Inn, Nevern

The Walk

From the village centre walk back across the bridge over the River Nyfer.

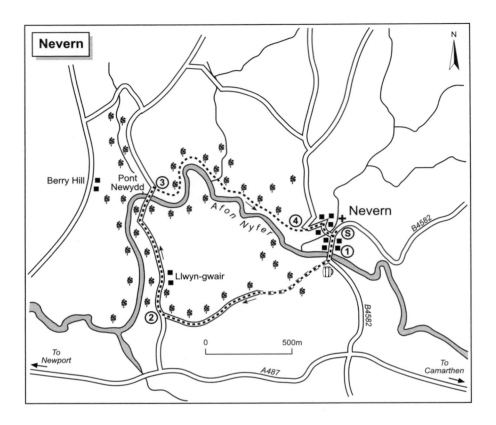

1. Immediately after the bridge turn right through a signposted gate to cross a field on a broad grass track, soon rising past a waymarked stile into the woodland of the valley side. At the top of the rise continue along a lovely lane between hedgebanks rich in wild flowers. In Spring, primroses, lesser celandine, wood anemones, ransoms and bluebells are all prominent. Go through a waymarked gate; the woodland is attractively mixed. In view to the left is the prominent rocky peak of Carn Ingli.

2. After a stile/gate join a very minor road. Turn right to follow the gently rising road. Below left is a large caravan site; pass derelict farm buildings on the right. One hundred and fifty metres after the buildings the road goes to the right. Bear left here at a signpost

Above: Mounting Steps
Below: Cletic Cross

and a 'Pont Newydd' sign. The broad unsurfaced track descends gently to the bridge. Cross the bridge.

3. In a further 70 metres, in front of a house, fork right to follow a signposted footpath, initially rising gently along the lower edge of the valley side. Pass a ruined cottage and continue by the side of the river. Ascend a short flight of rock steps before descending again to river level. Pass to the left of a house, cross its access drive, go over a little footbridge, cross another roadway and rise to a gate. Bear right at once to follow

the direction indicated by a waymark, across a field. Go over a stile and wind through the woodland of the valley side. There are sections of narrow path and more rock steps before a waymarked stile is reached. Go over and keep to the right hand boundary of a large field for the longest ascent of the route. Go over a stile in the top right corner. Continue towards the public highway, passing the ancient pilgrims' cross (signposted) cut into a rock face on the left.

4. Join the road, turning right to return to the village centre.

Walk 2: Gwaun Valley

This easy circuit has very little ascent. The outward route is on generally good woodland paths, with a return along the quiet valley road. There are few stiles.

The Gwaun Valley is an attractive and peaceful backwater. The River Gwaun rises high on the slopes of the Presceli Mountains and has cut a deep trough on its way to the sea at Lower Fishguard. Villages and hamlets in the valley are all small and well away from the usual visitor activity.

Distance	5 km (3 miles)
Ascent	35m (115ft)
Maps	Ordnance Survey Explorer OL35, North Pembrokeshire, 1:25,000
Start/Parking	Small car park (Allt Pontfaen) Immediately before the bridge across the R. Gwaun (when approached from Fishguard), grid reference 024340
Refreshments:	Dyffryn Arms Inn at Pontfaen

The Walk

Leave the car park by the signposted and obvious track at one end, skirting along the bottom edge of the wooded valley side. In spring there are plentiful wood anemones. The River Gwaun is soon close on the left, with the buildings of the linear village of Pontfaen across the valley. Parts of the otherwise excellent track are a little muddy and there are two small diversions to the right, both waymarked.

1. Behind Dan Coed Farm, the path rises then falls abruptly for a few metres to reach a wooden footbridge across a tributary stream. Cross the bridge. In about 50 metres keep left at a fork, over a stile. The path is now permissive, again basically level, along the foot of woodland.

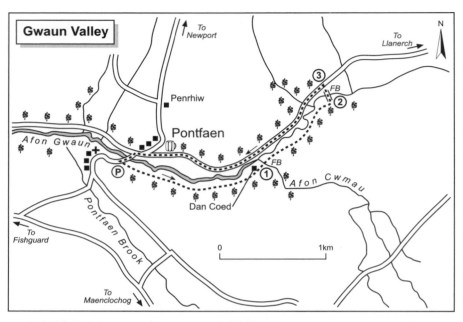

Bridge in the Gwaun Valley

2. In a little more than half a mile after Dan Coed reach a signposted junction. Turn left here towards Sychbant, over a stile, to cross a meadow. There are tree stump steps before a wooden footbridge across the river is reached. Cross and go over two more stiles to join the very quiet valley road.

3. Turn left to walk by the roadside, rich in wild violets, to Pontfaen village. Pass the Dyffryn Arms Inn, go straight ahead at a road junction, fork left at another junction in 40 metres and cross the river on the road bridge to return to the car park.

Walk 3: Llanwnda

This excellent circuit has more ascent than most of the walks in the book. Typical rise and fall along the Pembrokeshire Coast Path is followed by a steady but not steep return uphill to Llanwnda across farming land. With the exception of a short length of the outward route, all paths are good underfoot and are easy to follow. Several stiles.

Although quite close to the modern settlement of Goodwick and to Fishguard, the scattered hamlet of Llanwnda, on the upland of the promontory which includes Strumble Head, has a distinctly remote atmosphere. There is a charming little church which has surviving medieval wooden beams over the nave. Llanwnda parish has the remains of several dolmens, whilst nearby Garn Fawr is crowned by a striking stone hill fort.

Llanwnda Church interior

The area's chief claim to fame, however, is altogether more bizarre. On 22nd February, 1797, an expeditionary force of four ships, carrying 1400 soldiers from revolutionary France, the 'Black Legion', landed at Carregwastad Point, having failed to enter Fishguard harbour. The objective was presumably to start a revolution, 'liberating' the local population and eventually marching on London. The men were dressed in British uniforms captured during an earlier abortive raid on France. The ships returned to France and the expedition commander, Colonel Tate, set up his headquarters at Tre-Howel Farm. The events of the following two days, some actual and some unsubstantiated legend, could have graced the stage in a comic opera. The French troops scoured the area for food and drink. Finding considerable quantities of wine from a recent shipwreck, many soon decided that fighting was not a high priority and there were substantial desertions. In the meantime, a few local people and French soldiers had been killed in skirmishes, the alarm had been raised and Lord Cawdor of Stackpole had mobilised the Castlemartin Yeomanry, marching north, gathering extra troops on the way, to confront the invaders. His forces arrived at

Fishguard on the 23rd. The French were deployed on the cliffs above Goodwick. In the gloom confusion reigned and, following the misinterpretation of a drum signal, both sides retreated. To add to the confusion, groups of local women, dressed in red cloaks, were mistaken by the French as British grenadiers. One local woman is claimed to have marched into battle armed with a pitchfork and to have captured twelve French soldiers single handed. Unsurprisingly, Colonel Tate decided that he should sue for peace; terms were agreed and the documents were signed at the Royal Oak in Fishguard on Friday, 24th February. The curtain fell on the last invasion of Britain as it ended tamely with the French soldiers being escorted to imprisonment at Haverfordwest.

The events of this historic episode are recorded by a vivid thirty metre tapestry on display at Fishguard Town Hall.

Distance	7 km (4¼ miles)
Ascent	120m (394ft)
Maps	Ordnance Survey Explorer OL35, North Pembrokeshire, 1:25,000
Start/Parking	Informal space in Llanwnda hamlet, grid reference 933395
Refreshments:	None

The Walk

At the parking area are two 'public footpath' signposts. Carefully follow the indicated line, across the front of a house to a little path and a waymarked stile. Cross a field. Go over a waymarked stile and keep a hedge on the left. There are more stiles, mostly waymarked, as the same line is followed across two fields. After a signpost the path is better defined. After yet another stile bear right along a farm roadway, now very close to Ciliau Farm. Go through a farm gate, then left along the Ciliau access road.

1. Close to the Ciliau entrance turn right through the **second** of two waymarked gates to follow a little sunken lane, possibly cattle-churned. Go over a stile to rise past gorse and bramble. Pass a

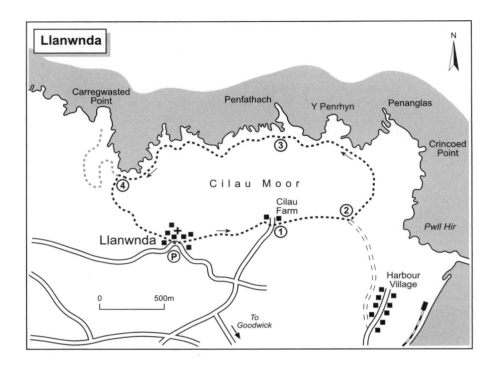

house, Carcoed, then turn left along a broad track descending gently towards the coast.

2. Join the Pembrokeshire Coast Path. Turn left. For some distance the path is broad and easy but after leaving the National Trust area of Pen Anglas there are descents and ascents more typical of the coast path. The scenery is superb as the route passes behind Anglas Bay and Porth Maen, with the peninsula Penfathach jutting out to sea.

3. A boggy area is passed on stepping stones before the path passes a signpost, with a track on the left leading back to Ciliau Farm (*a short return to Llanwnda if required*). Carregwasted Point comes into view across the great bay of Aber Felin. Descend to cross a succession of small plank bridges over streams tumbling to the sea below. Descend a flight of steps and continue up a flight of steps opposite.

Llanwnda Church

4. Twenty-five metres after passing through a little gate look out for a signposted stile on the left. Go over and follow the indicated line across a rising field towards Llanwnda, in view ahead. There is a waymark on a post in 100 metres then another, before a waymarked gate is reached. The route is never in doubt, including a farm access lane after a waymarked gate. Continue to rise along the now very obvious route into Llanwnda hamlet and the car parking area.

Walk 4: Strumble Head

There are no prolonged or difficult ascents, just the fairly frequent rise and fall which is consistent with the coast path. The inland return route is largely along an old drove way, with some muddy sections. The return finishes along the Strumble Head access road, entirely pleasant and with little traffic. There are several stiles.

The fine lighthouse in a dominant position at Strumble Head was built in 1908, at the same time as Fishguard harbour. There is no public access to the lighthouse which is operated automatically. Strumble Head is a noted place for bird watchers, with Spring and Autumn migrations of sea birds.

Distance	5 km (3 miles)
Ascent	70m (230ft)
Maps	Ordnance Survey Explorer OL35, North Pembrokeshire, 1:25,000
Start/Parking	Parking area at the end of the road leading to the Strumble Head lighthouse, grid reference 894412
Refreshments:	None

The Walk
Walk back along the access road, over a cattle grid.

1. Turn left through a waymarked gate (Pembrokeshire Coast Path). Continue to rise, passing the inevitable gorse. For a short distance the path is quite narrow and rough underfoot. The coastal views are attractive and extensive. The unmistakable path, now on short grass, passes a waymark on a post and behind rocky bays, Pwll Bach and Pwlluog before reaching the larger bay of Porthsychan, with its shingle beach. There are several stiles and the occasional gate, with primroses, violets and ancient field walls along the way.

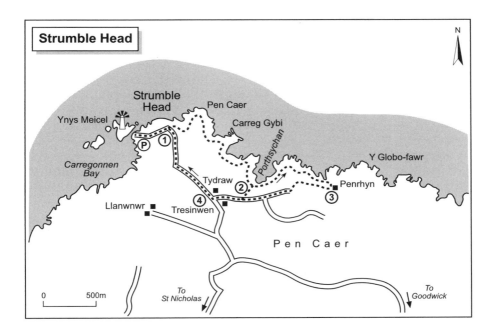

Descend to a plank bridge, where a little stream falls steeply down to the bay.

2. At a signposted gate there is a junction of tracks. *(A right turn here provides a short return to Strumble Head).* Turn left to continue along the coast path; cross a waymarked bridge and go uphill to a stile. Cross two more bridges and go over more stiles. The isolated house, Penrhyn, comes into view. Go through a gate to reach a junction, 100 metres before the house.

3. Turn right, towards a gate. Do not go though the gate; take the path to the right, on the nearside of an old wall. The path is generally clear on the ground, but one short section is a little overgrown; a minor diversion to the right is recommended here. The path

Hamlet near Strumble Head

Strumble Head Lighthouse

soon improves. Go straight ahead at a signposted junction with bridleway waymark; the track now assumes the character of an old drove way, muddy in places, heading for the visible hamlet at Tydraw. To the left the rocky mounds of Garn Gilfach and Garn Fawr are prominent. Go straight ahead at a signposted junction, cross a small stream, pass another signpost and rise gently to a gate to reach the hamlet in front of a bungalow. Turn left to join the Strumble Head access road.

4. Turn right to walk by the roadside, initially rising gently, to return to the car park.

Walk 5: Abercastle and Trefin

The section of the Pembrokeshire Coast Path which comprises the outward part of this route has an average amount of rise and fall, the most significant being close to the start of the walk. The return route, across farming country, uses established rights of way, some sections of which are not easy to follow on the ground and may be obscured by crops.

Abercastle is a lovely little hamlet of colour-washed cottages, a former sea port, nestling at the back of its narrow bay.

Trefin is a substantial inland village, open and windswept, with inn and tea shop.

Carreg Samson is one of the two finest Neolithic monuments in Pembrokeshire, a Cromlech or burial chamber readily accessed beside the return path.

Distance	9 km (5½ miles)
Ascent	105m (345ft)
Maps	Ordnance Survey Explorer OL35, North Pembrokeshire, 1:25,000
Start/Parking	Parking area, with public conveniences, behind beach at Abercastle, grid reference 853337
Refreshments:	Tea rooms and the Ship Inn at Trefin

The Walk

Start through a gate along the coast path, a lovely harbour-side terrace, soon passing above an old lime kiln. Across the harbour, Ynys y Castell is an island at high tide. Cross a concrete bridge, pass a signpost and gate to go left up a flight of steps, the most significant ascent of the route.

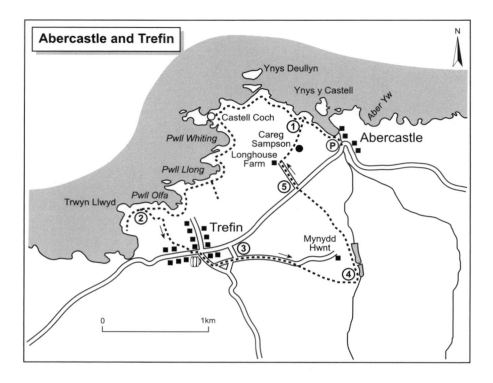

1. At a junction at the top go straight ahead to follow the coast path. There is a section where the path is not entirely clear over grass, but, overall, the way is never in doubt; just keep the sea to the right! Go through a gate and continue across an area of level grass to reach another gate and a marvellous viewpoint; to the right is the headland, Pen Castell-coch, the large bay is Pwll Whiting. The large village of Trefin comes into view to the left. There are more gates and the occasional sharp drop and rise. Cross a plank bridge at the bottom of one descent, the path here being rough underfoot. The next large bay is Pwll Olfa. Go through more gates and along the edge of a cultivated field. After a gate the path apparently forks; go right here to reach a signpost in a few metres.

2. Turn left towards 'Trefin ½ mile' to follow a good broad track towards the village, entered through a modern housing development, Heol Crwys. At the main street turn left. (*The Ship*

Inn is to the right). In 40 metres fork right for Croes Goch, downhill *(for a short return to Abercastle avoiding the rural ramble, go straight on at the fork, along the Abercastle road. This short cut reduces the overall distance by about one mile).* Pass the village hall and the hostel, then turn left along a track before the road begins to rise. In a short distance join another road, going ahead.

3. As this road rises and bends to the left go straight ahead, along an unsurfaced road, between hedgebanks. At a signposted fork turn right to leave the lane through a waymarked farm gate. Stay close to the hedge on the left of a large field. Go over a waymarked stile on the left. The right of way now goes diagonally across the next field to a waymarked ladder stile in the far corner. After the stile the indicated route is straight across the next large, cultivated, field; depending on the state of the crop, many walkers might prefer to detour, staying close to the field boundary on the right.

4. Reach a stile with a waymark on its far side. Do not go over; turn left before the stile to walk along the field boundary, above light

Abercastle Bay

woodland, soon passing a waymark on a post and above two small reservoirs, with Mynydd-hwnt Farm to the left. Go over a waymarked stile and up a bank to the left to reach a waymark on a post. From this point the right of way is diagonally left, a little to the west of north, across a huge cultivated field, possibly aided by tractor tracks. Alternatively walk along the edge of the field, above a little valley. The next objective is a waymarked ladder stile over a cement-rendered wall, reached either directly or with a left turn if the edge of the field route has been followed. From the ladder stile the obvious route is a farm track, straight ahead to reach the Trefin to Abercastle road.

5. Turn left for 100m at the road, then right to follow the Longhouse Farm access road. A signpost points the way round the farm, to the right. The superb cromlech Correg Sampson is soon reached. Continue gently downhill, past a waymark, to a gate. Go through, then straight ahead to rejoin the outward route at a gate, point 1. Turn right to descend the steps and return to the car park.

Walk 6: Abereiddy and Porthgain

A lovely section of the Pembrokeshire Coast Path is combined with a track across the headland, through Barry Island Farm, to make a good circuit. A section of the Porthgain access road is included. The three ascents are firstly at the start of the walk, secondly along the road from Porthgain and finally up the Barry Island Farm access track. None are really steep or difficult underfoot.

Both Abereiddy and Porthgain have an industrial history, commencing in the early part of the 19th century. At Abereiddy, without a harbour, the output from the slate quarry was taken to Porthgain by a tramway constructed along the valley behind Barry 'Island'. The lovely 'Blue Lagoon', now open to the sea, is the former quarry. Quarries close to Porthgain area yielded slate and, later, stone for road construction. Clay and slate waste were utilised for the making of bricks. By the early 20th century the industries had declined, leading to closure in 1931. During the relatively short period of operation the harbour was constructed and later improved, facilitating the export of large quantities of slate and stone, great storage hoppers for different sizes of stone were built on the hillside above the harbour and substantial buildings for brickmaking were erected, with railway lines connecting the various parts of the enterprise. The main industrial railway line, with steam locomotives, was at the top of the hill above the storage hoppers, with an engine shed and a crushing plant. The

Distance	6 km (3¾ miles)
Ascent	85m (279ft)
Maps	Ordnance Survey Explorer OL35, North Pembrokeshire, 1:25,000
Start/Parking	Large parking area, with public conveniences, behind the beach at Abereiddy, grid reference 797313
Refreshments:	Sloop Inn and The Shed teashop at Porthgain (both a small diversion from the suggested route)

ruins of many of these industrial buildings, with surviving quarrymen's cottages, are still evident, giving Porthgain a unique ambience.

The Coast Path passes behind the cove, with the lovely sandy beach, Traeth Llyfyn. As this beach is comparatively remote, reached only on foot from Abereiddy, Porthgain or via Barry Island Farm, it is unlikely to be crowded.

The Walk

Head for a gate at the northern end of the car park. To the right is a National Trust information board and the gaunt remains of a row of former quarrymen's cottages 'The Street'. Continue by ascending a short flight of steps. (*These can be avoided by walking to the right, past the front of the ruins, then turning sharp left to start up the surfaced path*).

1. At the top of the steps turn left to follow a rising surfaced path. In a few metres bear right at a signpost to continue the ascent along

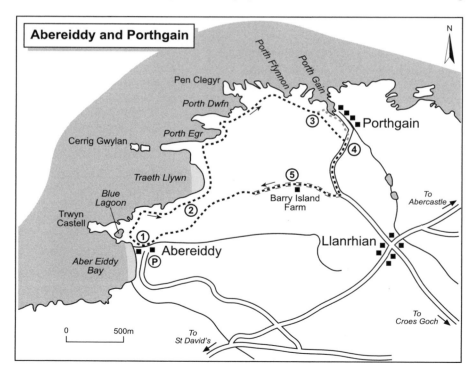

Porthgain Harbour

the Pembrokeshire Coast Path, soon passing high above the celebrated 'Blue Lagoon'. The fine grass track ascends gently, with an abundance of gorse and a rock outcrop before another bay is passed. There are long views back to the great outcrops of Carn Llidi, near St David's and the closer Carn Penberry.

2. At a gate with signpost a path joins from the right. Continue along the coast path, always very clear on the ground. Pass the top of a flight of steps leading down to the beach at Traeth Llyfn. Pass another gate and across the back of another rocky bay; in this area the field walls are of considerable antiquity. After yet another bay, the first remnants of the great Porthgain industry are apparent, with an obvious cutting to the left which formerly carried one of the industrial railway lines.

3. At a major waymarked fork our route bears to the right; (*to descend to harbour level at Porthgain and for refreshments bear left – this diversion adds a little to the overall ascent*). A good track stays with

the line of the railway, soon passing the remains of the brick structure which was the locomotive shed. Behind is the huge hole of the former main quarry. Go through a gate and follow the clear path, soon descending towards a large house, Ynys Faen. Pass the house to join the Porthgain access road.

4. Turn right to walk by the roadside, gently uphill, for a little less than half a mile to a junction. Turn right to follow the private road towards Barry Island Farm (Ynys Barry), crossing the (much obscured) line of the former tramway connecting Porthgain and Abereiddy. Bear right at the foot of the slope for a steady ascent towards the farm.

5. Pass a house on the right and keep straight ahead, to the right of the holiday cottages. Pass through a spacious farm yard to reach a waymarked gate. Continue along a broad lane; at a signposted fork go left through a gate and keep to the left edge of the field. After the next gate, descend towards the now visible Abereiddy beach along a good but possibly cattle-churned track. Close to the public

Cottages, Abereiddy

conveniences, descend to the left to a waymark on a post. Go through a gap in a wall and pass the near end of the public convenience block Go through a waymarked gate to return to the car park.

Walk 7: Whitesand Bay

This circuit starts along the Pembrokeshire Coast Path, with a return by footpath, quiet road and farm tracks. By the standards of the coast path, the rise and fall is very modest. The most significant ascent is from Porthselau, not prolonged and at an easy gradient. This section may well have some mud.

Whitesand Bay has the most extensive sandy beach of the St David's peninsula, a glorious swathe between wide-spaced rocky headlands. Inland, the bleak expanse of Trefeidden Moor provides contrast, with the impressive bulk of Carn Llidi the dominant landscape feature.

Distance	5¼ km (3¼ miles)
Ascent	85m (279ft)
Maps	Ordnance Survey Explorer OL35, North Pembrokeshire, 1:25,000
Start/Parking	Large (pay) car park at Whitesand Bay, with café and public conveniences, grid reference 734272
Refreshments:	Café at Whitesand Bay

The Walk

Start along the Pembrokeshire Coast Path, passing the front of the lifeguard building before rising gently towards an isolated house. The views are superb, with Ramsey Island visible beyond the headland in front, St David's Head away to the right and the great sweep of the sandy bay. Join the unsurfaced access roadway to the house, bearing right.

1. In less than 100 metres, at a signpost close to a bungalow, turn right to continue along the coast path. Apart from a few steps and a short rise, this is a generally level section of the coast path. Static caravans come into view ahead as the lovely little cove and beach,

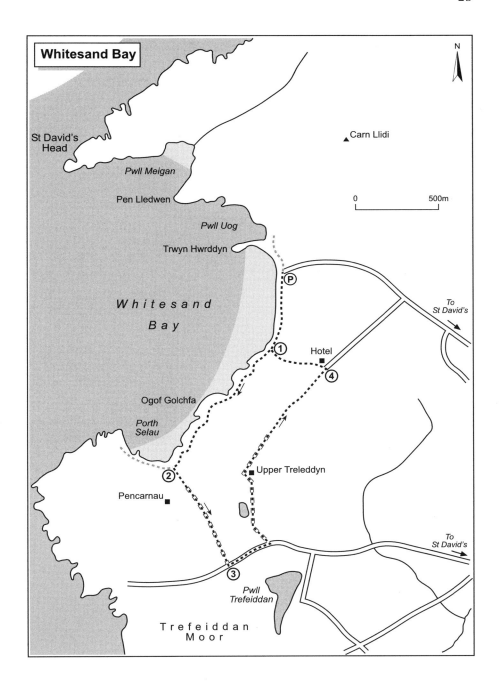

Whitesand Bay

N

St David's
Head

Carn Llidi

Pwll Meigan

Pen Lledwen

0   500m

Pwll Uog

Trwyn Hwrddyn

P

W h i t e s a n d

B a y

To
St David's

Hotel

Ogof Golchfa

Upper Treleddyn

*Porth
Selau*

Pencarnau

To
St David's

Pwll
Trefeiddan

T r e f e i d d a n
M o o r

Porthselau, is approached. Descend to a signpost behind the beach.

2. Turn left to rise gently along a grassy path alongside a little stream; there are some muddy sections but the path is easy to follow. Go diagonally right, then right at the top of the path to join a broad, unsurfaced, track leading to the caravan site access roadway. Go straight ahead along the roadway to reach the public highway. This area is Trefeiddan Moor.

3. Turn left to walk by the roadside for 300 metres. As the road bends to the right, turn left at a signpost to head for Treleddyn along a private access road. Pass a large pond, with waterfowl, soon reaching the sizable Treleddyn farmstead. Go straight through the farm, noting the (replica!) burial chamber. At the far end of the farm fork right at a signpost to head along an unsurfaced lane between hedgebanks towards the great rocky mass of Carn Llidi. Pass between a pond and an isolated house before reaching the Whitesand Bay Hotel.

Whitesand Bay

4. Turn left at a signpost before the hotel and its tarmac road to follow a broad private roadway descending gently towards the sea. Rejoin the outward route at point 1, turning right to return to the car park.

Walk 8: St David's

The only significant ascent is at the start of the walk, a rough path up the side of the valley by Porthclais harbour; otherwise, the route is easy, without stiles, and good underfoot.

The coast in the St David's area is magnificent; numerous rocky coves, sea cliffs crowned with gorse and swathes of wild flowers, all overlaid with a great sense of history, adding character to the windswept landscape, watched over by high outcrops of ancient rock such as Carn Lliddi. Bronze and Iron Age men were here, followed by saints in early Christian times; St David was reputedly born close to the village which carries his name and the well dedicated to his mother, St Non, is on the line of the walk set out below. Generations of farmers and fishermen followed, building the tiny harbours, burning the limestone in the still-evident kilns and constructing the ancient bankings which separate so many of the fields.

St David's itself is little more than a big village, but with the status conferred by the cathedral. It is an important centre for north Pembrokeshire, with shops, inns, cafes and the ruins of the former Bishop's Palace.

The short walk set out below forms a good introduction to the area, including a fine section of the Pemrokeshire Coast Path linking the bays of Porthclais and St Non's, with footpath connections to and from St David's.

Distance	5¼ km (3¼ miles)
Ascent	70m (230ft)
Maps	Ordnance Survey Explorer OL35, North Pembrokeshire, 1:25,000
Start/Parking	Car park with public toilets at Porthclais, 1¼ miles south-west of St David's, grid reference 740242. Follow the 'Porthclais' signs from St David's
Refreshments	Inns and cafes in St David's. Occasional kiosk at car park

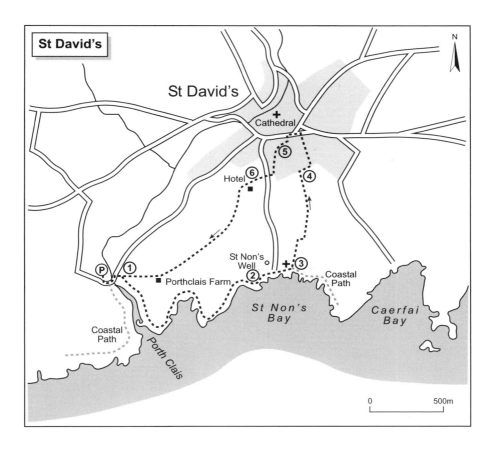

The Walk

Turn left out of the car park and cross the bridge over the stream.

1. Turn right to follow the 'coast path' sign, soon rising steeply to the left, with rough steps and some rocky surface. The track soon levels, winding its way above the spectacular scenery of the great sea cliffs; particularly impressive is the wild bay of Porth Ffynnon.

2. At a junction before the path descends to St Non's Bay, turn left through a gate, to cross a meadow on a grass track, heading for the ruin of the ancient St Non's Chapel, allegedly the birthplace of St

St Neon's Well

David. Continue to another gate, giving access to St Non's Well. Pass the well and then pass below a retreat centre. The modern (1934) St Non's Chapel can be visited by a short detour to the left. Carry on along the path, soon rejoining the coast path.

3. Turn left immediately at a 'St David's ½ mile' signpost to follow a clear track, heading inland. The path is well-organised between fences and old field boundaries, with modern gates.

Porthclais, National Trust Sign

Boats at Porthclais

4. At a 'T' junction at the fringe of the built-up area turn right. In a further 50 metres turn left at another junction, with signpost and seat, to head for the heart of St David's. At a road 'T' junction turn left, slightly downhill. At a junction in 100 metres turn right. In 50m. turn right again at a junction with a more important road, opposite the Tabernacle, to reach the focal point of St David's, with all facilities close by.

5. Commence the return by walking back past the Tabernacle, turn left into Mitre Lane, then turn right at a junction in 40 metres Follow this road for a short distance to the start of a bridleway along the edge of the built-up area, with a long terrace of bungalows on the left. Turn right at a junction, cross the minor road which leads to St Non's, with signposts each side, and continue.

6. At a fork with seat and 'N.T. Bryn Y Garn' sign, keep right, descending along a narrow path with a hedge/bank on the right. There are waymarked gates and the path is always clear to

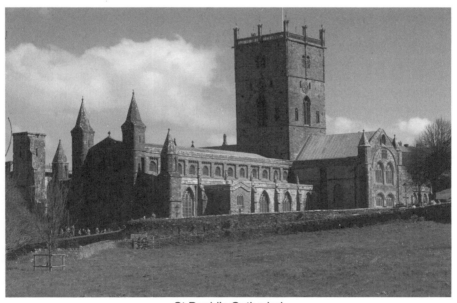

St David's Cathedral

Porthclais Farm, with a static caravan site adjacent. Follow the footpath signs through the farm and keep close to the field boundary on the right to head for a gate. The path across the next meadow is just visible on the ground. Pass a waymark on a post, go straight ahead at a cross-paths and descend the valley side on a steep but good path, aided by a few steps. Join the road, turning left to cross the stream and return to the car park.

Walk 9: Broad Haven

An attractive path from Broad Haven to Haroldston West, rising along a wooded valley, is combined with a section of the Pembrokeshire Coast Path to make a good circuit. The link between the two does involve some distance (less than one mile) along the side of minor roads. The ascent along the valley is quite prolonged but is nowhere steep or difficult, although there may be some mud.

Broad Haven is understandably popular, a wide bay defined by cliffs either side with an excellent sandy beach. The village has a general store, beach shops, inn and café.

Haroldston West is an ancient settlement, a tiny hamlet with a church much refurbished late in the 19th century.

Distance	6½ km (4 miles)
Ascent	120m (394ft)
Maps	Ordnance Survey Explorer OL36, South Pembrokeshire, 1:25,000
Start/Parking	Large pay and display car park with public toilets at the north end of Broad Haven village, entered from the road which leaves Broad Haven in the direction of Haverfordwest, grid reference 861140
Refreshments	Choice in Broad Haven

The Walk

Look for a signpost near the top left corner of the car park, pointing the way along a path by the side of the Youth Hostel.

1. Start along this path, passing the coastguard rescue station on the left. Bear left at another signpost. Pass an access to a static caravan site, do not cross a bridge on the left but go through a waymarked

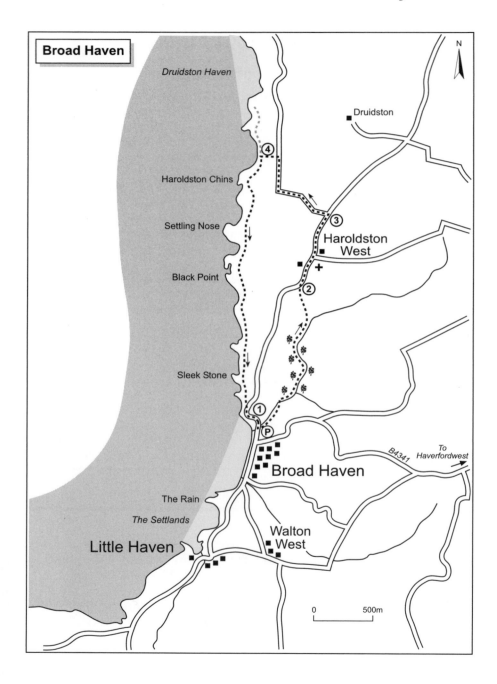

kissing gate to continue, with the stream on the left. The path follows the wooded valley, soon crossing the stream on a footbridge before rising steadily up the valley side. The woodland is very natural, with a good range of deciduous trees and abundant wild flowers, including bluebells and primroses in Spring. There are occasional mud patches along the way and marshy areas rich in irises. Ignore a signposted left turn near the valley head, continuing along the main path, soon passing Timber Hill Holiday Chalets to the right.

2. At a 'T' junction just before Haroldston West Church turn left to go through a gate and join a minor road. Turn right, passing a road junction and the entrance to Haroldston Farm. Walk by the roadside for less than half a mile to the next junction.

3. Turn left for 'Druidston Haven' to follow an even more minor road, soon with views over St Bride's Bay. Go round a sharp right bend to reach a small car park provided for disabled people, with a 'Haroldston Chin' sign. Turn left, through a gate, to take a tarmac

Broad Haven

surfaced footpath towards the sea. In a short distance join the coast path. There are seats provided for enjoyment of the splendid views.

4. Turn left; the path is tarmac surfaced for a few hundred metres. Follow the path; there are occasional gates and, possibly, grazing horses along the way. At a signposted junction continue along the coast path, soon reaching outlying dwellings of Broad Haven. The descent is quite prolonged but well graded, close to a road for some distance. Join the road, descend to cross the bridge and turn left along a footway into the car park, passing the public toilets.

Walk 10: Mill Haven

Distance	6 km (3¾ miles)
Ascent	80m (263ft)
Maps	Ordnance Survey Explorer OL36, South Pembrokeshire, 1:25,000
Start/Parking	Informal area, with public conveniences, at St Bride's Haven, grid reference 803109
Refreshments:	None en route

St Bride's Haven

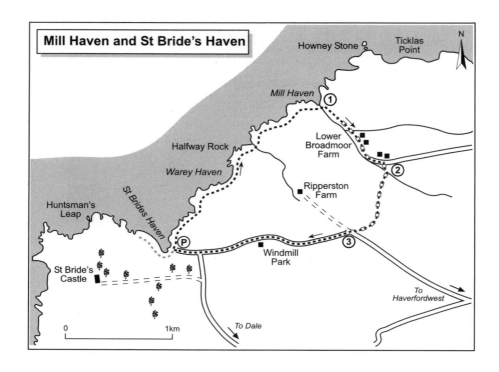

An excellent length of the Pembrokeshire Coast Path leads from St Bride's Haven, close to St Bride's Castle, to Mill Haven, a little cove further along the coast of St Bride's Bay. The inland return route is on good tracks via Lower Broadmoor Farm, with approximately one mile along the side of the minor road which leads to St Bride's Castle. If walking along the road does not appeal, the alternative is an out and back walk to Mill Haven. The total ascent is fairly average, mainly on the section rising from Mill Bay to Lower Broadmoor Farm, neither steep nor difficult.

The coastal scenery is very fine, including long views to the north coast of St Bride's Bay, with Ramsey Island, on a clear day.

The Walk

At a coast path signpost follow a track which leads to the beach, with a lime kiln to the left. Go down a few steps and keep to the right edge of the rock and shingle, crossing a little stream. Pass Cliff Cottage on its seaward side, rising to a gate. Follow the unmistakeable coast path above several bays, enjoying the views. There are occasional gates and a stream is crossed on a bridge. Spring flowers include gorse, primroses, sea campion and thrift. The impressive rocks just off shore are the Stack Rocks. Pass a sculpted rock with a hole before descending to Mill Haven. There are the remains of stone structures, including a lime kiln, but no apparent evidence of a former mill.

1. Cross the stream on the substantial bridge. At a signpost immediately above the lime kiln turn right, through a gate, to follow a track rising inland, between the gorse. Pass a signpost and go over an ancient stone stile to follow a lane leading to Lower Broadmoor Farm; there is a pond below, right. Pass between the farm buildings to reach the farm access road; there is a footpath sign by the wall on the left.

2. In about 400 metres there are huge agricultural buildings to the left and a house on the right. Just beyond the house turn right, at

St Bride's Castle

a signpost, to follow a broad track, descending initially with woodland on the right. This track soon rises to join the St Bride's Castle access road at another farm building.

3. Turn right to walk by the roadside. As the road bends to the left in just under one mile, go ahead to return to the car park

Walk 11: Marloes

A varied circuit combining the delightful St Bride's Haven, a length of the Pembrokeshire Coastal Path, Musselwick Sands and Marloes village. In addition to the rise and fall which is average for the coast path, there is a steady, but not too steep, ascent from behind Musselwick Sands to the Marloes road. The route is well waymarked and is easy underfoot. There are several stiles, some of them of traditional stone construction.

The coastal views are extensive, past the Stack Rocks to the distant north shore of the vast St Bride's Bay and also to the nearer Martin's Haven and Wooltack Point to the south-west.

Marloes is an attractive linear village, with church, chapel, inn, restaurant, shop and public conveniences.

Distance	8km (5 miles)
Ascent	110m (361ft)
Maps	Ordnance Survey Explorer OL36, South Pembrokeshire, 1:25,000
Start/Parking	Informal area, with public conveniences, at St. Bride's Haven, grid reference 803109
Refreshments	Lobster Pot Inn and Clock Tower Restaurant, Marloes

The Walk

From the car parking area start along the track behind St Bride's Haven; to the right is an old lime kiln and fragments of coffins from an earlier monastic burial ground. Pass picnic tables, cross a stream and go through a little gate. The path is very clear, with good views to St Bride's Castle. Pass a beautifully sited seat. Pass through the extensive estate wall at another gate; note the white acorn waymark of the coastal path. The path winds its way along the top of low sea cliffs punctuated with steep, narrow, coves, predominantly sandstone,

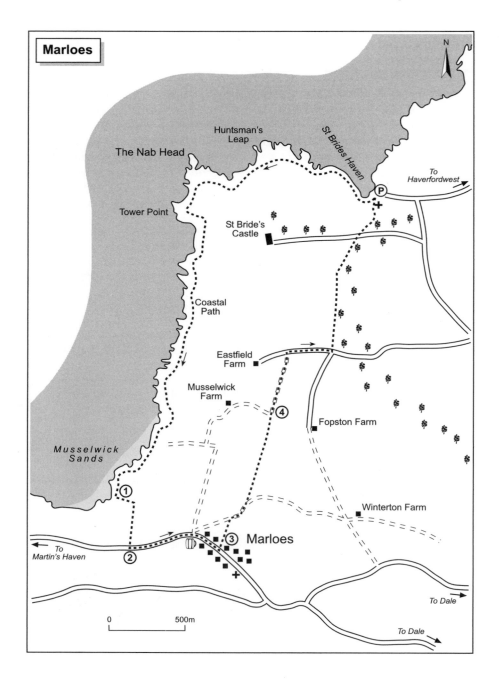

lined with a lovely selection of flowers – bluebells, primroses and the blazing yellow of the gorse. There are stiles and a gate before a three way signpost is reached as Musselwick Sands is approached. Go straight ahead for 'Marloes', passing a picnic table.

1. The path bears to the left, inland, joining tracks rising from Musselwick Sands, below right, at a signpost. There is a tiny stream on the right. Rise to another signpost in a short distance and continue along the edge of a field, with a hedge/bank on the left, rising gently to a gate at the top.

2. Join a minor road, turning left to walk by the roadside to Marloes village.

3. At Moriah Baptist Chapel, opposite the Lobster Pot, turn left (*the restaurant, the Kensington Clock Tower and the shop are a little further along the village street*). At a signpost in 20 metres go through a kissing gate by the entrance to 'The Fold'. There is another kissing gate, then a path along the left edge of a field. After

Marloes

another kissing gate join a farm track, turning right. In a little more than 100 metres leave the farm track in front of a house, through a waymarked kissing gate. Continue along the left edge of a meadow, go over a stile and along the left edge of the next field; Fopston Farm is to the right. After a kissing gate, turn left in 100 metres to go over the hedge/bank by a waymarked stile and a few steps.

4. Join a cart track, turning right, down the edge of another field; Musselwick Farm is prominent to the left. Turn right at a 'T' junction at the bottom, along a farm lane. Ignore the first path on the left; as the lane bends to the right, go over a stile on the left to follow a path along the edge of woodland, over several traditional stone stiles and along the bottom edge of several fields. Go through old kissing gates to cross a lane and continue to the bottom of the drive leading to St Bride's Castle. Go across and take the path leading through the St Bride's churchyard to the parking area.

left: Kensington clock, Marloes

Walk 12: Martin's Haven

Lengths of the Pembrokeshire Coast Path beyond Marloes are linked by a cross country route to provide an excellent circuit, first rate underfoot, with modest ascent and with minimal stiles. The short final part of the walk, up the steep little road from the Haven to the car park is the most demanding ascent.

Martin's Haven is the embarkation point for boat trips to Skomer; there is a small exhibition centre and public toilets behind the cove, and an important inscribed stone. Beyond St Martin's, the 'Deer Park', almost an island, extends towards Skomer, providing the best mainland viewpoint for that island. There have never been deer on this headland, but the substantial boundary wall is evidence of the intentions of the then landowner. (The deer park has footpaths which circle the headland and divert to Wooltack Point. These can readily be added as an extension to the route set out below.)

The views enjoyed on this walk embrace lovely coastal scenery, including the islands of Skomer, Skokholm and Gateholm.

Distance	6¼ km (4 miles)
Ascent	60m (197ft)
Maps	Ordnance Survey Explorer OL36, South Pembrokeshire, 1:25,000
Start/Parking	National Trust car park at Martin's Haven, grid reference 761090
Refreshments	None en route; Call at Marloes village on return for an inn and a café

The Walk

Start through the little gate at the bottom left corner of the car park, along a track on the right edge of a field.

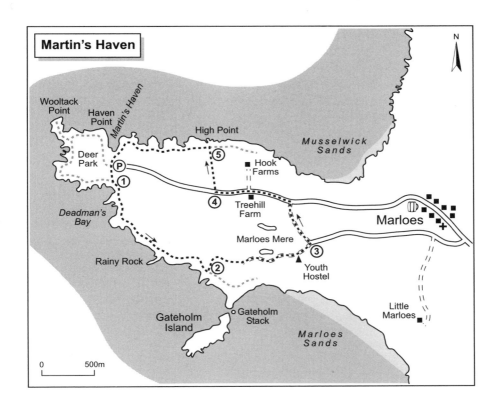

1. Go through another gate to join the coast path, turning left. The fine coastal scenery includes Skomer and Skokholm. Continue on the excellent path just inland of the top of the cliffs for approximately one mile.

2. At a signpost fork left, through two gates, to follow a fenced track. Go through another gate and cross a ditch before turning left at another signpost to keep to the left edge of a field. After the next signpost there is a gate and the start of an unsurfaced lane. Along the lane, look out for a bird hide to the left, overlooking a pool. Pass a 'car park' signpost and the youth hostel before joining the public road by the entrance to the National Trust Marloes Sands car park.

3. Turn left to walk through the car park, continuing along a broad track at the far end to reach the Martin's Haven access road. Turn left to walk by the roadside for just over a half mile, passing Treehill Farm.

4. Turn right to leave the road at a signpost, over a high stone-stepped stile. Walk along the left edge of the field towards the sea. There is a gate/stile and a left/right/left manoeuvre before the coast path is reached, over a stile.

5. Turn left to follow the path above the cliffs and coves back to Martin's Haven, reached down a long flight of rough steps. Turn left to ascend the road back to the car park.

Inscribed stone, Martin's Haven

Walk 13: Dale and St Ann's Head

This comparatively long walk follows the Pembrokeshire Coast Path around the peninsula adjacent to the village of Dale, visiting St Ann's Head and various bays en route. Overall the coastal scenery is very fine and, as usual on the coast path, the route finding is easy. There are several stiles and some flights of steps; the total ascent is reasonable, with significant rises at the three bays on the outward part of the route.

Dale is a pleasant village, situated on the large estuary known as Dale Roads, with strong emphasis on sailing and other water-based pastimes. Nineteenth century fortifications, guarding the entrance to Milford Haven, were constructed at Dale Point and West Blockhouse Point; the former is now a field studies centre. At St Ann's Head, a coastguard complex included lighthouse and cottages, now in private ownership.

Distance	11¼ km (7 miles)
Ascent	130m (427ft)
Maps	Ordnance Survey Explorer OL36, South Pembrokeshire, 1:25,000
Start/Parking	Pay and display car park in Dale village, grid reference 611059
Refreshments	Inn and café in Dale

The Walk
From the car park turn right along the roadside, passing the café and the Griffin Inn.

1. At a road junction go straight ahead to follow the tarmac road heading for 'Field Centre'. This road is part of the Pembrokeshire

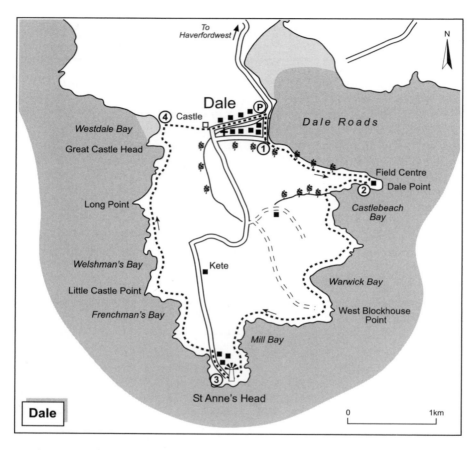

Dale

Coast Path. Approaching the field studies centre in about three quarters of a mile, look out for a gate on the right, waymarked with the coast path acorn.

2. Turn right here to take a grass path cutting across the back of Dale Point and then around the huge Castlebeach Bay. After Watwick Point is Watwick Bay, with an expanse of sand. At West Blockhouse Point are navigation towers and the remains of more fortifications. After descending steps and crossing a boardwalk over the stream at Mill Bay rise up steps to a waymarked gate, soon passing a plaque on a rock commemorating the landing of Henry Tudor on 7th August 1485. Approaching StAnn's Head, with its proliferation

of houses and other buildings, pass below the first terrace of houses, alongside a wall on the left and cross a meadow, rising towards another row of houses. In front of these houses, bear right to follow the fence to a gate and signpost.

3. Turn right, along the tarmac road, passing a former lighthouse, now a private dwelling. After passing a residents' parking area turn left at a well-marked gate to continue along the coast path. After Frenchman's Bay, pass a 'National Trust Kete' sign and continue along the cliff tops, with superb coastal scenery. There are great banks of sea thrift, gorse, primroses and other wild flowers along this length of the path. Hayguard Hay Farm is to the right, behind a large bay, before the descent to Westdale Bay, with its fine beach, is commenced. There are views right across the peninsula, including Dale village. The descent includes a long flight of steps.

4. Behind the beach turn right, over an old stone stile, to walk along the bottom of a meadow towards the village. Go through a little gate to join an unsurfaced road. Go straight ahead to join the

Slipway, Dale

public highway, passing Dale Castle, then the church of St James the Great. Turn right at a junction with the main Dale road to return to the car park.

Walk 14: St Ishmael's

This short circular walk is based on the rather scattered village of St Ishmael's, including Monk Haven and a delightful length of the Pembrokeshire Coast Path, with a return through part of the village. Most of the ascent is on the coast path as it rises from Monk Haven, with a lesser ascent after passing through the village.

St Ishmael's has an interesting old parish church with Norman font, a shop and an inn.

Monk Haven is a small cove backed by a huge former estate wall. Between the Haven and the church is Monkhaven Manor, nestling in its richly vegetated sheltered valley.

Distance	3¾ km (2¼ miles)
Ascent	80m (263ft)
Maps	Ordnance Survey Explorer OL36, South Pembrokeshire, 1:25,000
Start/Parking	Informal parking area in the woodland close to the church at St Ishmael's, grid reference 831068
Refreshments	Brook Inn in St Ishmael's (or the coffee shop at the garden centre on the fringe of St Ishmael's)

The Walk

Turn left from the car park, passing through the gateway to Monkhaven Manor. There is a 'to the coast path' sign. Pass the church and round the back of the manor house, which is close on the left. The woodland in this lovely little valley is carpeted with the flowers of ransoms and bluebells in early spring.

1. Reach the coast path at the back of Monk Haven, a pebble beach protected by a huge, formerly battlemented, wall at the back. Turn left to cross the stream and ascend steadily along the path, with

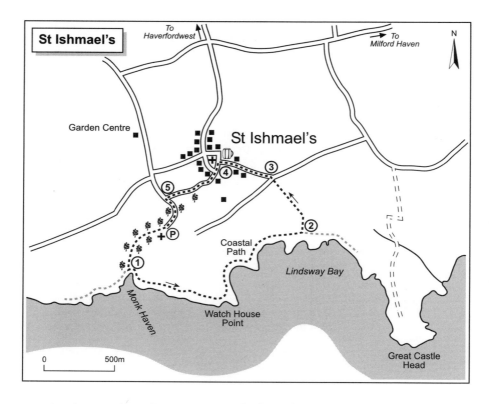

ever-improving views, soon including the St Ann's Head peninsula
and the village of Dale. Pass a ruined stone watch tower and
through a little gate. The path continues behind Watch House Point,
where there are the remains of World War II structures, and along
the tops of impressive cliffs. Great Castle Head is the headland
prominent ahead. Go through a waymarked gate.

2. At a signpost turn left to leave the coast path along a tarmac
   surfaced path at the right edge of a huge field. Pass along the edge
   of the village sports field and through a play area, with public
   toilets, to join a road.

3. Turn left, along the second road, not the cul de sac, to walk by the
   roadside towards the village centre. Pass the school and go straight
   ahead, downhill, at a junction to reach The Brook Inn, to the right.

Dale village from coast path

4. If not visiting the inn, turn left at the nearby junction to continue along the road, with a stream on the right. Go straight ahead at the next junction, uphill, away from the village.

5. Turn left at a 'T' junction to follow the access road back to the car park.

Lookout tower, near St Ishmael's

Walk 15: Angle

With a modest amount of ascent, largely at the start, this is a relatively undemanding route. A straightforward section of the Pembrokeshire Coast Path is combined with less than one mile by the side of a minor road to complete the circuit. For much of the walk the views are dominated by the busily commercial estuary of Milford Haven.

On the southern side of the estuary, very much off the beaten track, Angle is a pleasant village of modest size, with church, inn and shop. Within the village are the ruins of several medieval structures – The Tower House, a dovecote and the so-called Nunnery. The parish church of St Mary has a 14th century tower, a 15th century fishermen's chapel and a tiered 'preaching cross' in the churchyard.

West Angle Bay has a lovely sandy beach; adjacent is a chimney which was part of a brick works, also an ancient graveyard, being steadily eroded by the sea. East Angle Bay is notable for the expanse of mud flats exposed at low tide, a great feeding area for a variety of

East Angle Bay

birds, and for the remote Old Point House Inn, allegedly the haunt of smugglers in previous centuries. For obvious reasons, coastal defence has been an important issue around the mouth of Milford Haven since the late16th century when Henry VIII had two towers built. The Napoleonic wars and the late 19th century saw further construction, including a substantial fort at Chapel Bay, with internal moat. A substantial blockhouse survives on Thorn Island.

Distance	6½ km (4 miles)
Ascent	55m (181ft)
Maps	Ordnance Survey Explorer OL36, South Pembrokeshire, 1:25,000
Start/Parking	Large free car park, with public conveniences, behind the beach at West Angle Bay, grid reference 855032
Refreshments	Two inns at Angle, beach café at car park

The Walk

Leave the car park by the obvious unsurfaced roadway at the far end, with a 'coast path' signpost, passing above lime kilns and rising gently towards a headland. There are views over the bay towards St Ann's Head at the tip of the Dale peninsula.

1. In about 150m. fork left to leave the roadway along a signposted footpath. Fork right at once to continue along the coast path, still rising gently. The great blockhouse on Thorn Island is close on the left as the path bears to the right, with long views across the great natural harbour of Milford Haven. Dale Roads, St Ishmael's, Stack Rock and the various refineries and oil tanker terminals are all in view. The path is entirely clear and easy to follow, with any rise and fall very slight and gentle. Pass the remains of Chapel Bay fort. Cross the access track to the fort. There is a lightly wooded section with hawthorn blossom, bluebells, campion and other flowers along the way in Spring. Pass several waymarked gates as the path

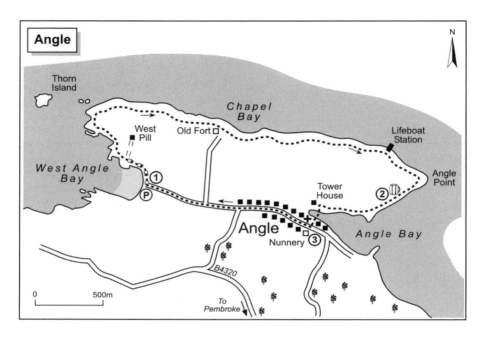

keeps to the edge of meadows and cultivated fields. Continue above the modern lifeboat station, then across its access road, on the descent towards Angle Point.

2. Shortly after passing the Point reach the car park of the Old Point

Old Point House, Inn, Angle

House Inn, an ancient hostelry, where there is an information board Pass the inn and continue along its unsurfaced access roadway by the shore of East Angle Bay, with great expanses of mud flat at low tide providing food for a range of waterfowl. Approaching Angle village, to the right is

Angle Church

the ruin of the medieval Tower House. Cross a bridge over a little stream to join the village street.

3. Turn right to walk through the village, passing the church, public conveniences, the ruins of the 'Nunnery' (to the left), the village shop, an information board, the colonnaded and battlemented former Globe Hotel and the Hibernia Inn. Leave the village, continuing by the roadside back to West Angle Bay.

Walk 16: Bosherston and St Govan's Chapel

The walking is generally easy, with the coast path from Broad Haven as the only significant ascent, largely over soft sand. The final part of the circuit is along the St Govan's access road, with little traffic and good roadside verges.

The great lily ponds at Bosherston are one of the showpieces of the South Pembrokeshire coast. Coupled with the adjacent Broad Haven and, by the Pembrokeshire Coast Path, with St Govan's Chapel, they make a walking circuit of considerable interest, with varied and attractive scenery.

The lily ponds are three sizable lakes, all linked, created as estate enhancements by the late 18th/early 19th century landowner. There are bridges facilitating the circular walks around the ponds, all very visitor-friendly.

Broad Haven is a beautiful wide cove and beach, with the Pembrokeshire Coast Path passing behind. Further along the coast St Govan's Chapel is a remarkable survival. Founded in the 6th century by the eponymous saint, most of the present structure dates, at the latest, from the 13th century. The real wonder of the chapel is its location, clinging to the side of steep limestone cliffs above the sea, accessed only by a long flight of steps.

Distance	6½ km (4 miles)
Ascent	70m (230ft)
Maps	Ordnance Survey Explorer OL36, South Pembrokeshire, 1:25,000
Start/Parking	National Trust car park, with public conveniences, behind Bosherston Church, grid reference 967948
Refreshments	St Govan's Country Inn and Ye Olde Worlde Café (seasonal) at Bosherston

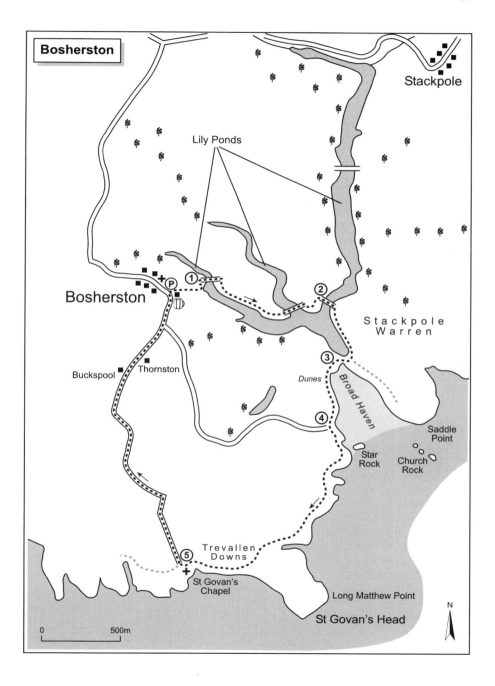

The large area known as Castlemartin ranges is used by the army for gunnery practice. This area, which includes St Govan's Head and Chapel, is closed to the public when in military use. The boundaries are clearly marked and red flags are displayed on these occasions. (Should this occur, a shortened version of the circuit can be made by turning sharp right behind Broad Haven to follow the footpath along the south-western side of the ponds directly back to the car park.) For up to date information, enquire at a Tourist Information Centre or telephone 01646 662287.

The Walk

From the car park descend along a well-made track towards the lily ponds, the left hand of the two descending paths.

1. Turn left at the junction at the bottom and bear right to cross the first long footbridge, with a coast path waymark. The path continues to the right, close to the water; above to the left, in impenetrable vegetation, is an iron age fort. Go up a few easy steps; to the right at a fork is a short diversion to an excellent viewpoint.

Broad Haven, near Bosherston

Ancient cross, Bosherston

Resume along the main track, go down easy steps and cross the second footbridge. At Middle Arm keep right at a signposted junction for 'Broad Haven'. Wild flowers in Spring include bluebells, primroses, violets, gorse and bugle.

2. At a signposted junction follow 'Broad Haven' at Grassy Bridge. Turn right to cross the bridge over the eastern arm. The track now passes along the edge of the extensive Stackpole Warren, with a luxuriant reed bed on the right. Ignore the coast path to the left at a signpost and continue to the back of the Broad Haven beach. Cross the stream on a waymarked footbridge to head for a signpost in 100m. *(If the track across the firing range is closed, a sharp right turn is required before reaching the signpost).*

3. The signpost offers two ways ahead, diverging only slightly. Keep left at a fork in 50m. Continue over sand to rise along one or other of the obvious routes; there are many possible variations, but the objective is to reach the top edge of the slope, with great views over the Haven and out to sea. Quite suddenly the path turns inland, up

steps or ramp, to a signpost and Broad Haven car park, with public conveniences.

Historic AA sign, Bosherston

4. If the range is open, continue along the coast path, passing a waymark on a post and through a gate. Pass the range checkpoint; there are frequent white posts along the broad easy track and warnings of the danger of straying off route. Stay with the main coast path at any apparent junctions. Turn right at a signpost to go over tarmac to a waymarked gate and cattle grid. There are more signposts as the St Govan's car park is reached. The short left diversion to visit the chapel is signposted.

5. From the coast path turn right, inland, to walk past the car park and along the quiet access road, passing range buildings. The roadside banks are rich in flowers; in Spring the cowslips are particularly impressive. Pass a long-abandoned cottage and leave the range at the Newton hut. Pass a farm; Bosherston Church is soon in view. Reach the edge of the village, continuing towards the church, passing the inn and the cafe. At the junction in front of the church turn right to return to the car park

Walk 17: Manorbier

An excellent section of the Pembrokeshire Coast Path is combined with inland lanes, footpath and short lengths of quiet road to form a circuit of modest length. There are several stiles but no problems with walking surfaces. The ascent includes an initial rise from the car park to Manorbier village and fairly typical rise and fall along the coast path. Manorbier Castle is one of the great defensive structures built by the invading Normans in the 12th/13th centuries. The castle was provided with mills, dovecote and fish pond, the remains of some of which can still be seen. Unlike most of the Norman castles in South Wales, it was never attacked by the native Welsh.

The church of St James, with a striking high tower of 1270, faces the castle across a shallow valley. Manorbier village is pleasant but unremarkable.

The route of the walk passes behind the splendid Presipe Bay, with sandy beach; towards the end of the walk is King's Quoit, a Neolithic cromlech, not common in the south of the county.

Distance	5½ km (3½ miles)
Ascent	80m (263ft)
Maps	Ordnance Survey Explorer OL36, South Pembrokeshire, 1:25,000
Start/Parking	Large car park, with public conveniences, almost opposite Manorbier Castle, grid reference 064977
Refreshments	Hotel in Manorbier village

The Walk

Leave the car park, turning right to walk up the side of the road towards the village.

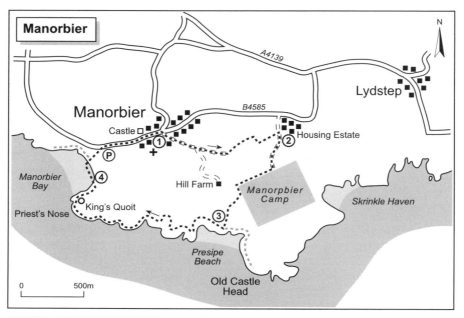

Manorbier Castle

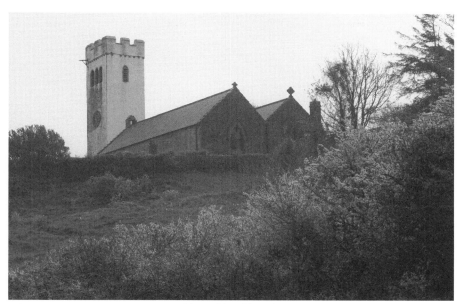

Manorbier Church

1. Turn right at the Castlemead Hotel, immediately after a road junction, to take a surfaced lane ('cul de sac'). After the last house the lane loses its hard surface; at a signposted fork go left to continue along another broad track. Pass an isolated dwelling, go over a stile and pass the remains of a lime kiln. At a signposted junction of paths go straight ahead on a good path. There are superb primroses in a dell on the left. Shortly after another stile turn left by a waymark for a short rise. Continue along the left edge of a field. In view to the right is a housing estate. Bear right at a signpost to head for the houses.

2. Go over a stile by a children's play area to join a road. Turn right, as indicated by a signpost, to walk by the roadside, gently uphill towards buildings. Just before the gates of the artillery range turn right, over a stile, to join the signposted coast path. Keep close to the security fence on the left to pass some of the buildings of the range. Go over a signposted stile at the far end of the buildings to turn left and head towards the sea; there is a signpost 100 metres ahead.

3. Go over a stile and turn right to follow the coast path, initially level but with some rise and fall ahead. Below left is the lovely beach of Presipe, which can be accessed down steep steps. The descent and ascent required to cross a deep little valley can be much reduced by detouring to the right immediately after a stile, initially keeping close to a field wall. Stay with the coast path at any junction. After the Priest's Nose headland, the extensive Manorbier beach comes into view. Reach the King's Quoit, a fine cromlech with the capstone collapsed at one end, before beginning to angle down towards the beach.

4. Go down a few rock steps to reach the beach. The coast path continues across the back of the beach; look out for a signposted right turn with a path leading directly to the car park.

Walk 18: Tenby and Penally

Tenby Harbour

This circuit, combining the coast path across the expanse of Tenby south beach with Penally village and a track beside the railway line is almost completely level, good underfoot, and can be recommended for all.

Tenby hardly needs description; a deservedly popular resort which has all facilities and a great deal of appeal for most visitors, including a good range of individual shops and cafes, but has nevertheless avoided the worst excesses of bigger and better known seaside towns.

Penally is quite different. Largely perched on a knoll overlooking the sea and by-passed by through traffic, the quietly attractive village has a popular inn and a 13th century Norman church. Inside are one complete and two broken Celtic crosses.

The Walk

From the car park head for the sea along a boat launching ramp.

Distance	4 km (2½ miles)
Ascent	Very little, perhaps 10m (33ft)
Maps	Ordnance Survey Explorer OL36, South Pembrokeshire, 1:25,000
Start/Parking	South Beach car park (pay and display), Tenby, grid reference 131001
Refreshments	Cross Inn, Penally; kiosk at car park

1. As soon as firm sand is reached turn right to walk between sea and sand dunes for a little more than one mile. Ahead are the rocks of Giltar Point, with Caldey Island to the left of the Point.

2. Turn right at a signposted short flight of steps to leave the beach. Follow a surfaced path passing a Tenby Golf Club notice. The attractive village of Penally is ahead. Stay with the main path at a signposted junction, pass one end of a rifle range and cross the railway line on a level crossing, close to Penally railway station. Cross over the Penally by-pass road, turning left then right to follow a little road rising into the village.

3. In a few metres turn right to walk along the road through Penally. (*The Cross Inn is a few metres to the left at this junction*).

Cottages, Penally

Cross Inn, Penally

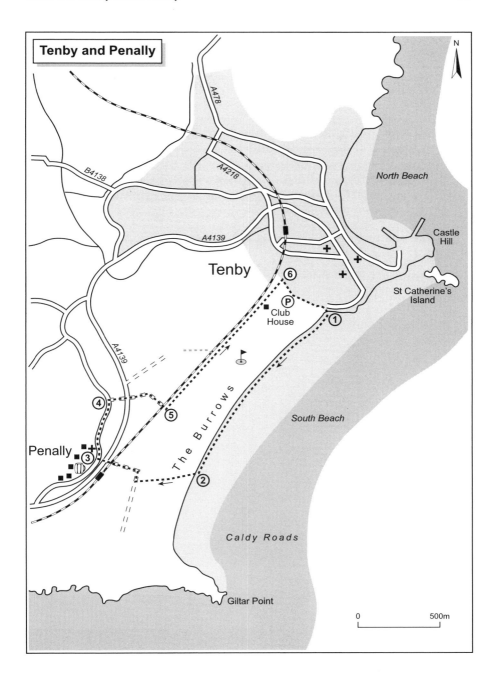

4. In about 400 metres turn right. There are two signposted footpaths here; take the nearer, along a rough surfaced road past the old school. Cross the by-pass road to a broad track opposite with a Pembrokeshire Coast Path sign. Cross a bridge and continue towards the sea.

5. Cross the railway on another level crossing, turning left immediately along a path close to the railway line, rich in wild flowers. As a track joins from the right, bear left to rise to a signpost close to a railway bridge. Go straight ahead, now along a surfaced roadway sandwiched between the railway and the golf course. Pass the golf clubhouse.

6. As the roadway rises, fork right to follow a signposted footpath leading directly to the car park.

Penally village

Walk 19: Saundersfoot

A mini walk, short, entirely level and on firm surfaces throughout, the trackbed of a former railway line, entirely pleasant and undemanding. Some walkers might appreciate the use of a torch in the longest tunnel. The views are over beaches of sand and rock to the promontory, Monkstone Point. A return to Wiseman's Bridge may be made by the use of the coastal bus service (approximately every two hours – timetables at the Tourist Information Centre in Saundersfoot) or by walking back along the outward route.

Wiseman's Bridge is described in walk number 20.

Saundersfoot is a popular small resort with many individual shops, cafes and restaurants, It has a fascinating industrial past, becoming a busy port in the 19th century serving, mines and collieries from the areas of Kilgetty, Stepaside and Wiseman's Bridge. Of great importance was the 4ft gauge railway (or 'tramway'), officially opened in 1834, linking collieries in the Kilgetty and Stepaside areas with Saundersfoot. The trucks were initially pulled by horses, but later in the century steam power was introduced.

Beach, Saundersfoot

Distance	(One Way) 1¾ km (1 mile)
Ascent	Negligible
Maps	Ordnance Survey Explorer OL36, South Pembrokeshire, 1:25,000
Start/Parking	Roadside parking at Wiseman's Bridge, mostly close to the Wiseman's Bridge Inn, grid reference 146061
Refreshments	Wiseman's Bridge Inn. Wide choice in Saundersfoot

Tunnel at Saundersfoot

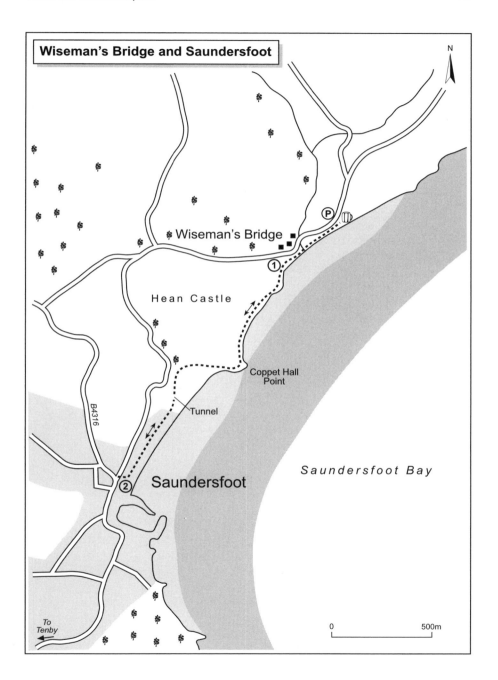

Wiseman's Bridge and Saundersfoot

N

Wiseman's Bridge

Hean Castle

Coppet Hall
Point

B4316

Tunnel

①

② Saundersfoot

P

Saundersfoot Bay

To
Tenby

0   500m

The Walk
Head along the coastal road, away from the Wiseman's Bridge Inn.

1. Cross the bridge then, as the road bears to the right, rising, fork left along a wide surfaced track which follows the line of the long defunct mineral railway. The level walkway is along the base of a steep cliff and above the fine and extensive beach. The first and longest tunnel is soon reached. Go through; at the far end Saundersfoot comes into view. Next is a short tunnel, followed by a large car parking area, with a hotel to the right. Cross the area towards public conveniences. The route continues past the end of the conveniences, entering the third tunnel. After the tunnel continue along the Strand towards the centre of Saundersfoot. This was formerly Railway Street, with the line running along the middle of the road on its way to the harbour.

2. The Tourist Information Centre, behind the harbour, is at the heart of Saundersfoot. The bus stop is a little further; after a right turn into Milford Street, the stop is on the left, about 50 metres from the harbour car park entrance.

Walk 20: Wiseman's Bridge

The former industrial railway line connecting Saundersfoot, Wiseman's Bridge and the Kilgetty ironworks at Stepaside makes a splendid outward route. Recently enhanced, this broad, almost level track follows the well wooded Pleasant Valley. The return involves a fair amount of ascent of the valley side before heading back to Wiseman's Bridge along a very minor road. (Alternatively, the outward route can be used for an entirely easy return.)

Wiseman's Bridge is a minor settlement behind an extensive beach; in the 19th century the extraction of coal (high quality anthracite) and iron ore was the basis of a thriving local industry. The railway line originated in 1832, being extended in 1842. Initially the trains were horse drawn, the first steam locomotive being acquired in 1874. By 1939, the coal industry was finished, with the line being dismantled shortly after World War II.

There are substantial remains of the Kilgetty iron works, now preserved as an industrial heritage site, including casting shed, engine and boiler houses. Further up the valley side is the site of the former Grove colliery, also with an information board. During its short life, from 1856 to 1870, it produced anthracite of high quality; the shaft, at 640ft, is claimed to be one of the deepest in South Wales. Drainage problems brought about the early closure.

Distance	4 km (2½ miles)
Ascent	(circuit) 85m (279ft) (out and back) Negligible
Maps	Ordnance Survey Explorer OL36, South Pembrokeshire, 1:25,000
Start/Parking	Informal spaces behind the beach at Wiseman's Bridge, grid reference 146061
Refreshments	Wiseman's Bridge Inn

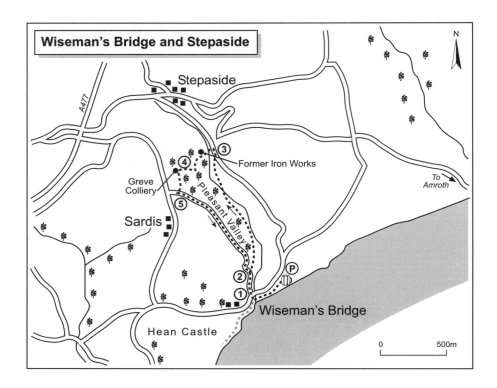

The Walk

Start along the road behind the beach at Wiseman's Bridge, heading away from the inn. Cross the bridge over the river.

1. Turn sharp right by a bus shelter to pass beside a house, following a tarmac lane, the line of the long defunct industrial railway.

2. At Tramway Cottage keep right; there is a bridleway sign 'Stepaside 1.14 km (0.71 miles)'. Pass a gate to continue along the former railway line, now a broad, easy, track, rising very gently through the woodland of the aptly named Pleasant Valley. The route stays generally close to a little river, with marshland supporting a range of attractive plants, including marsh marigolds and irises. Cross the river on a stone bridge. Pass a caravan site on the left before reaching a gate and joining the Pleasant Valley road.

Former Kilgetty ironworks

3. Turn left. Across the road is a beautifully restored former mill building. In 50 metres. turn left into the site of the former Kilgetty iron works, now an industrial heritage site. The remains, explained on an information board, are considerable. *(For the out and back walk retrace the outward route from the former iron works).* For the circuit continue past the ruins of the buildings to a flight of steps on the left. There are two flights of steps from the former iron works; either will serve to reach the next objective – the site of the former Grove Colliery. Ascend the steps to reach a broad track, higher up the wooded valley side. Turn left to walk, still rising, towards the colliery remains. There are several signposts.

4. The surviving colliery buildings, again with information board, are set in a clearing. Continue past the colliery, the path now narrower, rising through woodland to a stile.

5. After a second stile join a very minor road. Turn left to begin the steady descent back to Wiseman's Bridge. The sides of the road

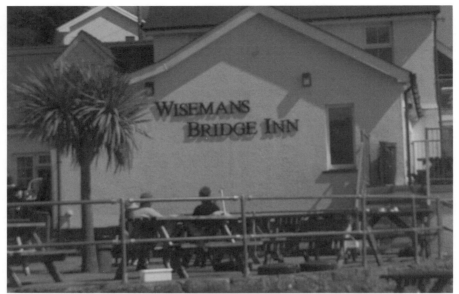

Wiseman's Bridge Inn

are rich in flowers, bluebells and primroses in particular. Pass several isolated houses. The sea comes into view before the steep descent to rejoin the outward route at Tramway Cottage. Turn right to return to the car park; a slight variation of path stays close beside the river, passing in front of the public conveniences.

Walk 21: Amroth and Colby Gardens

Overall, this walk has the greatest ascent. The start, along a section of the Pembrokeshire Coast Path, is by the roadside behind the huge beach, almost to the boundary with Carmarthenshire where the Path actually starts (or ends!). After turning inland there is quite a long rise through delightful woodland but the gradient is reasonable. The second notable ascent, after Eastlake Farm, is shorter but a little steeper. With the exception of a small area of possible churning by cattle, all tracks are good underfoot and there is only one stile.

Amroth is a small settlement tucked away behind a fine beach in the south-east corner of Pembrokeshire, with two widely separated inns and a handful of shops and cafes. It is now quite difficult to imagine Amroth as a busy 19th century industrial centre, with iron and coal both extracted nearby .

The parish church of St Elidir is on higher ground, three quarters of a mile inland.

Colby Gardens are attached to a private residence, Colby Lodge, but are open to the public, administered by the National Trust. In addition to a walled garden, there is an extensive woodland garden, with numerous footpaths available to visitors. The popular complex also includes an arts and crafts gallery, shop and café.

Distance	6½ km (4 miles)
Ascent	150m (492ft)
Maps	Ordnance Survey Explorer OL36, South Pembrokeshire, 1:25,000
Start/Parking	Large free car park behind the row of shops in Amroth, grid reference 162070 (or find a space along the sea front road)
Refreshments	Inn and cafes at Amroth; café/tea shop at Colby Gardens

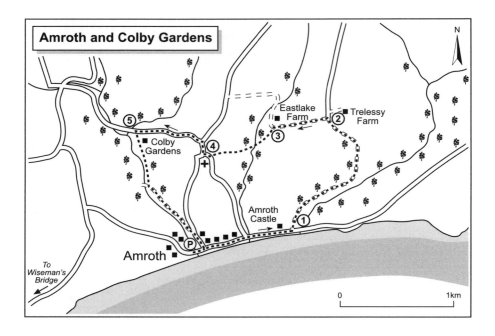

The Walk

Head east along the sea front road; there is a little 'promenade' beside the road for some distance. Pass the Amroth Arms Inn and the Amroth Castle caravan site.

1. Immediately after public conveniences turn left at a footpath signpost. Pass between two houses then bear right to another signpost to follow a bridleway, a broad easy track rising gently into woodland, rich in bluebells. Pass an isolated house before commencing the longest ascent of the route. There is a farm to the right and a stream on the left as the ascent of about 80 metres (263ft) continues. The track bears left before leaving the woodland. Go straight ahead at a junction, followed by a cross roads in a further 30 metres, with signpost and a farm to the right.

2. Turn left along the access drive to Eastlake Farm, over a cattle grid. Pass a house on the right and head for the farmyard. Look carefully for a waymarked left turn, through a narrow gap in a fence. Cross

a concrete farm track to a similar gap and turn right, along a narrow path for 30 metres. At the bottom follow the waymark indication to the left and continue round the back of a large cowshed.

3. Cross a cleared area to a waymark showing a left turn, along a wide, level, track into woodland. Descend gently to a wooden bridge over a stream. In a further10 metres turn right at a signpost to leave the broad track, following a narrow path rising through woodland. At the top of the rise go through a kissing gate to continue along a possibly cattle churned path at the bottom edge of a field. The tower of Amroth church comes into view ahead.

4. At a gate/stile join a minor road, turning right to walk past the church to a road junction. Keep right, passing a former school on the left. In 80 metres turn left at a road junction, signposted to Colby Woodland Garden. Follow the little road, downhill, passing the entrance to the Colby Gardens car park and beside a walled garden. Just past the walled garden is a signpost.

Colby Gardens

Refreshments at Colby Gardens

5. Turn left at the signpost to go through a gate and between the Colby Garden café/tea room and the walled garden. After an 'Amroth ¾ mile' signpost continue along a fine broad track, part of the designated 'Knights' Way' trail, at the bottom edge of valley-side woodland. Ignore any tracks to left or right. At a short terrace of houses, reach tarmac, descending to join a minor road. Bear right, soon reaching the right turn into the car park.

Walk 22: Carew River

Carew River

Most of the ascent in this walk is included in one gently graded rise starting close to the river and heading towards Paskeston Hall. The walking is entirely easy, although there is a distinct likelihood of mud, the worst sections being crossed on boardwalks.

The route is largely through attractively mixed deciduous woodland close by the side of the Carew River, making a change from the understandably popular coastal path. Close by, Carew Castle, Carew Tidal Mill and the Celtic Carew Cross provide an alluring concentration of visitor attractions (see walk 23).

The woodland is particularly rich in wild flowers – primroses, ramsons, celandine, bluebells and orchids are all present in Spring. The views include sections of the tidal river and, from the higher part of the route, Carew Castle and the Preseli Hills.

Distance	4¾ km (3 miles)
Ascent	40m (131ft)
Maps	Ordnance Survey Explorer OL36, South Pembrokeshire, 1:25,000
Start/Parking	Small roadside lay-by close to Ford bridge on the minor road connecting Milton with Cosheston, grid reference 029034. The lay-by is a little less than one mile from Milton along this minor road
Refreshments	None en route. Inns at Milton and Carew, nearby

The Walk

From the lay-by cross the tiny Ford Bridge, adjacent.

1. Twenty metres after the bridge turn right, over a stile. There is a signpost. Follow the clear path through the woodland. Go through a little gate. The path is never far from the tidal river; after passing an area of reed beds, there is a faint path deviating to the right to reach Hakin Point, with uninterrupted views up river towards the tidal mill. Continue along the main path, with little bridges and boardwalks easing the way past the worst of the mud. Look out for a lime kiln just to the right of the track. Go through another little gate before approaching a stile. Forty metres to the right is the long abandoned ruin of Paskeston Cottage.

Lime kiln, Carew River

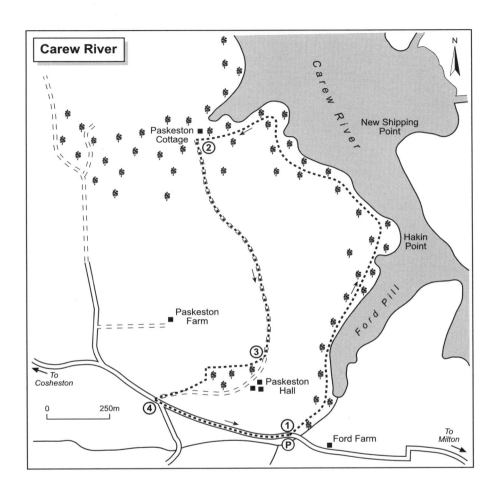

2. Go over the waymarked stile to leave the woodland, turning left, up the left edge of a meadow. Go straight ahead, rising between rows of mature trees to a gate/stile in the top corner. Carry on along a broad track, fenced on the right. From this highest part of the circuit Upton Castle is in view behind and Carew Castle can be seen through gaps in the hedge to the left. The distant hills are the southern part of the Preseli range. Pass woodland on the left before reaching a house. Go through a farm gate.

3. In 50 metres as the main track continues into the grounds of
   Paskeston Hall, turn right at a signpost, go through a waymarked
   farm gate and continue along the left edge of a large meadow, the
   path hardly visible on the ground, passing behind Paskeston Hall.
   After another gate at the top of the meadow, bear left to descend
   through woodland and join a Paskeston Hall access track. Turn
   right to walk past a lodge and reach the public road.

4. Turn left to walk by the roadside back to the parking place.

Walk 23: Carew Castle

Carew Castle

Distance	1½ km (1 mile)
Ascent	Negligible
Maps	Ordnance Survey Explorer OL36, South Pembrokeshire, 1:25,000
Start/Parking	Free car park close to the entrance to the castle, grid reference 046037. There are public conveniences across the road
Refreshments	Tea room at Carew Mill; Carew Inn

This circuit is a mini walk, accessible to all, truly level and very easy underfoot. Within its short compass are three outstanding features – the great medieval Carew Castle, perched serenely above the enormous mill pond, Carew Mill, one of only five restored tidal mills in Britain and an outstanding Celtic Cross, one of just three surviving examples in Pembrokeshire. The castle and the mill, the latter with its original machinery, are open to the public, daily from April to October.

The Walk

Turn left from the car park to walk along the little lane passing to the left of the castle. There is an information board by the entrance to the castle grounds.

1. As the road forks bear right towards the now visible tide mill, a splendid structure. Pass in front of the mill and continue along the

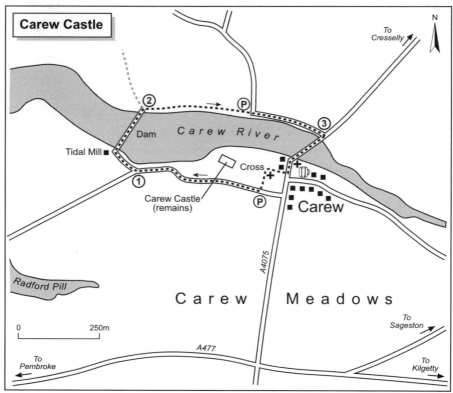

Carew Tide Mill

great causeway which holds back the water of the enormous mill pond providing the power for the mill.

2. At the far end of the causeway ignore the footpath signs; turn right to follow the path which has been created along the shore of the pond. Pass another car park/picnic area and join a minor road. Continue to the junction with the main road.

3. Turn right to cross the long bridge then rise a little, passing Carew Methodist Church before turning right, through gates. Bear left to rise past the Celtic Cross and return to the car park.

Walk 24: Lawrenny

*This popular circular walk is a little more difficult than might be
expected. The path through Lawrenny Wood is narrow, with a few
rocky steps. After rain it is also likely to be muddy, needing care. The
section of the route along the shore of Garron Pill, a minor creek off
the main estuary, may be under water at a very high tide. If in doubt
consult a tide table or check at the yacht station.*

*Lawrenny village is pleasant, with the 12th century church of St
Caradoc prominent and with a small general store.*

*In common with other villages around the great and complex
estuary of the Daugleddau, Lawrenny Quay had considerable use as
an industrial port, with cargoes mainly of coal and limestone and with
transhipping of goods to smaller vessels for access to some smaller
ports further inland. For the early part of the 19th century Lawrenny
was also second only to Milford in local shipbuilding. The later
development of quays further down the river, accessible to larger craft,
and the decline of the coal and limestone industries ended the trading
at Lawrenny late in the 19th century. The Quay is now a centre for
pleasure boating.*

Distance	5¼ km (3¼ miles)
Ascent	75m (246ft)
Maps	Ordnance Survey Explorer OL36, South Pembrokeshire, 1:25,000
Start/Parking	Large area at Lawrenny Quay, grid reference 011061
Refreshments	Lawrenny Arms Inn and Quaysiders Café (both at Lawrenny Quay)

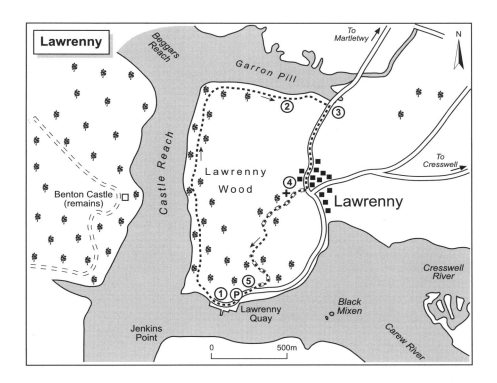

The Walk

Walk towards the Quaysiders Café, turning right, before the café, into a boat storage yard. At the entrance to the boatyard a signpost indicates a left turn, along a permissive path, part of the designated Landsker Borderlands Trail.

1. Go ahead, into woodland, with the Lawrenny Quay Caravan Park to the right. Pass another signpost, then turn right immediately before a gate, along a waymarked path through the continuous woodland. The water of the Daugleddau is visible below to the left. Go over a stile. The path, narrow and possibly muddy after rain and with a few rocky steps, continues for a little more than a mile, up and down, weaving among the trees, largely old oak, with the occasional wild service tree. The views across the estuary include Benton Castle, oddly coated in whitewash. Continue round the curve

Lawrenny Quay

behind Jenkins Point, the path now above Garron Pill, one of the minor creeks off the main estuary. There is a fine long view to the village of Llangwm.

2. Go over a waymarked stile and down a few steps to descend to the shore of the Pill. Turn right to follow a clear route, normally well above high tide level. Near the head of the Pill bear right on a broad track, with a fence on the right, to join a minor road at a signpost.

3. Turn right to walk by the roadside, uphill, to Lawrenny village.

4. Immediately after passing the entrance to the churchyard turn right, through a signposted kissing gate *(in order to avoid a further ascent of about 15m (49ft) – the minor road can be used as an easy return route. Turn right at the junction in a few metres).* For the recommended return, cross a little waymarked bridge after the

kissing gate and head for a gap in the hedge across the field. Keep to the right edge of the next field, with a stone wall on the right. Rise along the left edge of the next field, to a kissing gate near the top. Go through; there are splendid views down the estuary. Keep to

Café at Lawrenny Quay

the top edges of two fields, separated by a stile. Go through a kissing gate, with permissive path waymark, to continue between brambles, soon descending through woodland on a fine, wide, path.

5. Reach the road to Lawrenny Quay close to the Lawrenny Arms and the public conveniences. Turn right to return to the parking area.

Walk 25: Blackpool Mill

This circuit of medium length contains an average total of ascent overall, separated into several uphill sections, all being at gentle gradients and relatively undemanding.

Much of the outward route and some of the return route of the walk is through Minwear Wood, part of the Forest Enterprises Slebech Forest, high on the side of the river valley. Apart from some mud, there are no difficulties and very few stiles.

The very impressive four storey Blackpool Mill dates from the early 19th century. During that century substantial ships could deliver cargoes of grain along the tidal Eastern Cleddau River. The mill has been restored and is now a seasonal visitor attraction, housing a museum, with shop and tea room.

Distance	8¾ km (5½ miles)
Ascent	90m (295ft)
Maps	Ordnance Survey Explorer OL36, South Pembrokeshire, 1:25,000
Start/Parking	Car park at Blackpool Mill, grid reference 060144
Refreshments	Tea room at Blackpool Mill (seasonal)

The Walk

Start from a signpost in the car park at Blackpool Mill, immediately to the left of the toilets, along a grass path. Go through a gate with a permissive path waymark and cross a meadow to a waymarked gate/stile. Keep left at a signpost, cross a swampy area on a boardwalk to reach a gate/stile with a Landsker Borderlands Trail waymark. Rise into woodland.

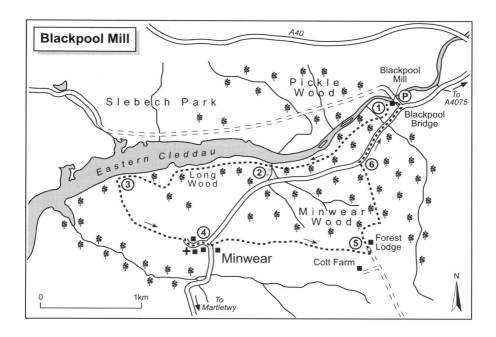

1. At a waymarked post turn right, along an unsurfaced roadway. Pass a wooden barrier and continue along a broad track through the attractive woodland. Cross a stream, rising to a junction. Go straight across; the river is below to the right and there is soon a short diversion to a viewpoint with seat, for a fine view of the valley, with extensive reed beds. Continue along the main path, now narrower but always clear on the ground. Go straight ahead at a signposted junction, descending to cross several little streams on footbridges.

2. At a cross-paths go straight ahead; there is a 'Minwear Woods – permissive path' sign. There are more footbridges and another rise before the path levels, high above the river. Bluebells and primroses are abundant in Spring. Cross another bridge before rising to a Landsker Borderland Trail waymarked post. Turn right here; along the way are posts with yellow tops.

3. Go over a stile, with adjacent railings. Bear left; close by are the ruins of 'Sisters' House', reputedly a hospice for female pilgrims

en route to St David's and St Non's Well. Rise along a sunken lane. After a modern kissing gate continue along the left edge of a field. At the top bear left at a gate/stile by the side of a pond. A farm lane leads through Minwear Farm to join a road beside a church. Follow this road to a junction with the public highway.

4. Turn right, then left in 20 metres to follow a broad track through two gates. This bridleway, a sunken lane, continues, gently uphill, for approximately one mile, passing through several modern gates. Some sections are likely to be muddy from use by horses. Cott Farm is in view to the right before a junction, with an unsurfaced road, is reached.

5. Turn left, soon reaching tarmac. Pass a farm, Forest Lodge, and carry on along a broad track descending gently through woodland. Reach rough tarmac and continue, ignoring any apparent junction. Pass a cluster of houses immediately before joining the public highway.

Blackpool Mill

6. Turn right; there is a path through the trees beside the road. Pass a road junction, staying with the major road, downhill, to the entrance to the Blackpool Mill car park. Turn left into the car park

Also available from Sigma

NORTH WALES WALKING

on the level

Norman and June Buckley

This is the seventh volume of the popular and well-established series of 'level walks' books. There are 30 walks covering an area from The Great Orme to Cemlyn Bay. Whilst walks in North Wales are treasured by those who love the mountains, the balance of the book is much enhanced by the inclusion of the Conwy Valley and the Lleyn Peninsula, both part of the wider definition of Snowdonia, and by Anglesey, its near neighbour.

£8.99

HOLIDAY WALKS IN NORTH WALES

Brian Conduit

20 walks ranging from 2 to 6 miles in length, all within the capabilities of most people, varying in difficulty and the nature of the terrain. The scenery is varied and magnificent and the walks vary from easy and flat riverside strolls to more challenging walks in the Snowdonia National Park or on the slopes of the Clwydian hills.

£8.99

ALL-TERRAIN PUSHCHAIR WALKS: SNOWDONIA

Zoë Sayer & Rebecca Terry

A superb collection of pushchair-friendly walks for North Wales. These 30 routes explore the spectacular scenery of the Snowdonia National Park – including an adventurous walk that takes you and a pushchair half-way up Snowdon! The walks range from simple riverside strolls to full-on alpine-style stomps.

£7.95

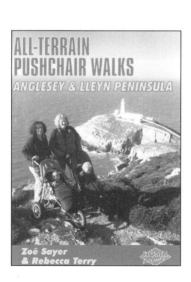

ALL-TERRAIN PUSHCHAIR WALKS: ANGLESEY & LLEYN PENINSULA

Zoë Sayer & Rebecca Terry

Pushchair walks by the sea — from beach strolls to cliff-top rambles. There are 30 tried-and-tested routes from simple beach strolls to rugged inland hill-top rambles through fields, woods and over hills and mountains with scarcely any obstacles and never any need to remove the child from the pushchair.

£7.95

WALKS IN THE FOREST OF DEAN AND WYE VALLEY
Dave Meredith

The Forest of Dean and Wye Valley is a paradise for both the keen rambler and the casual stroller. The 22 walks described in this book are along easy footpaths taking you to spectacular viewpoints, along woodland glades carpeted with bluebells, daffodils and foxgloves, and under the dappled shade of its golden autumn canopy. £8.99

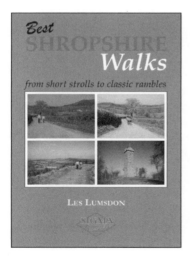

BEST SHROPSHIRE WALKS 2ND EDITION
From short strolls to classic rambles
Les Lumsdon

A new revised edition of this much loved guide contains 36 walks, including 12 completely new routes, located in all parts of the county. Several walks feature fine hill walking on the Welsh borders and others start from delightful villages and hamlets in the north and east of the county.

The Shropshire countryside really comes alive in this well-researched book. All of the walks include stories about the locality: folklore and legends, attractions and facilities. There are clear maps and a selection of photographs to make for an enjoyable and informative read. £8.99

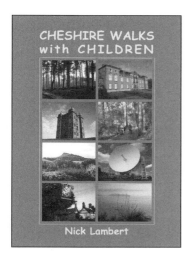

CHESHIRE WALKS WITH CHILDREN
2nd Edition
Nick Lambert

Now completely revised and updated, this was the first in our "walks with children" series and has quickly become a firm favourite. There are 30 walks, ranging in length, together with things to look out for and questions to answer along the way make it an entertaining book for young and old alike.

£8.99

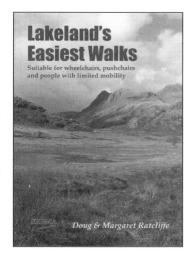

LAKELAND EASIEST WALKS
Suitable for wheelchairs, pushchairs and people with limited mobility
Doug & Margaret Ratcliffe

The Lake District and surrounding area has become far more accessible for wheelchairs and pushchairs in recent years. Although essentially a book for wheelchair users, these 38 specially selected short walks are all equally suitable for people with limited mobility and for very young children. Many of entries also have a 'points of interest' section describing features that can be seen from the paths and the photographs included illustrate the fact that a wheelchair or pushchair is no barrier to the wonderful Lakeland scenery.

£7.99

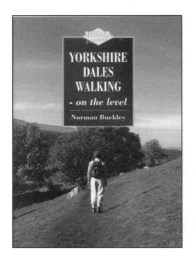

YORKSHIRE DALES WALKING
On The Level
Norman Buckley

This is a book for people who enjoy a relaxed approach to walking — walks that can be enjoyed whatever the weather. There are 32 walks without serious ascent which explore the heart of the Dales countryside and are packed with a wealth of interesting features encountered along the way. All the walks are based on well-known towns and villages, mainly within the most popular and best-loved Dales

If you're travelling by car to and from the relevant town or village, you'll appreciate the carefully selected and recommended car parking areas.

£7.95

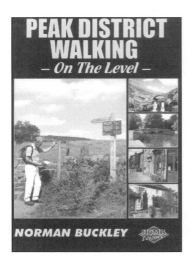

PEAK DISTRICT WALKING
On The Level
Norman Buckley

This is a book for people who enjoy a relaxed approach to walking — walks that can be enjoyed whatever the weather. The walks are ideal for family outings and the precise instructions ensure that there is little chance of losing your way. Well produced maps and inviting photographs encourage everyone to try out the walks.

The whole of the Peak District is covered — both the Dark Peak and the White Peak — with visits to such gems as Edale, Castleton, Eyam, Chatsworth and Bakewell.

£7.95

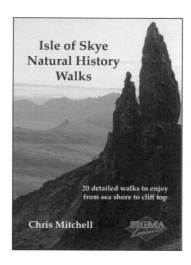

ISLE OF SKYE NATURAL HISTORY WALKS
20 detailed walks to enjoy from sea shore to cliff top
Chris Mitchell

An alternative guide to the wildlife and geology of Skye detailing where to see the island's lesser-known natural history. There are 20 walks based around Portree, Dunvegan, Broadford and Sleat together with detailed maps and quality photographs. Skye has long been regarded as a special place for the birdwatcher, the geologist, the botanist and marine biologist. By taking time to 'stand and stare' you will discover for yourself this hidden side of Skye – one that complements the traditional image of seascapes and mountain views. 70 colour photographs.
£9.99

THE CHARLIE CHAPLIN WALK
Stephen P Smith
This book is targeted at fans of Chaplin, those interested in film history, people with a connection to the Lambeth and Kennington areas of London and anybody with an interest of the social history of London's poor of the late Victorian and early Edwardian era. Explore the London streets of Charlie Chaplin's childhood in a chronological tour that can be taken on foot or from the comfort of an armchair. This book concentrates on the story of Chaplin's formative years and takes a fresh look at the influence they had upon his films.
£9.99

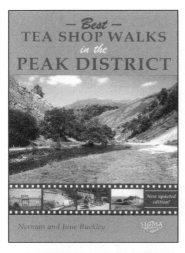

BEST TEA SHOP WALKS IN THE PEAK DISTRICT
Norman and June Buckley

A wonderful collection of easy-going walks that are ideal for families and all those who appreciate fine scenery with a touch of decadence in the shape of an afternoon tea or morning coffee —or both! The 26 walks are spread widely across the Peak District, including Lyme Park, Castleton, Miller's Dale, and The Roaches and — of course — such famous dales as Lathkill and Dovedale. Each walk has a handy summary so that you can choose the walks that are ideally suited to the interests and abilities of your party. £7.95

THE WATERFALLS OF ENGLAND
A practical guide for visitors and walkers
Griff J Fellows

This unique guide is aimed at all who enjoy walking, fine scenery and natural history – whilst discovering the beauty of the water-falls of England. From Northumberland to the southern tip of Cornwall there are nearly 200 wonderful yet easily accessible waterfalls to admire. Each waterfall is given a unique star rating for its attractiveness and appeal, together with clear directions, location maps and parking facilities – along with features of local interest.
£9.99

All of our books are available through booksellers.
For a free catalogue, please contact:

**Sigma Leisure, Stobart House, Pontyclerc
Penybanc Road, Ammanford SA18 3HP**

Tel: 01269 593100 Fax: 01269 596116

info@sigmapress.co.uk   www.sigmapress.co.uk